TALES FROM AN EX-HUSBAND

A Story of Survival, Betrayal, and
Other Shady Things

Harry Carpenter

CONTENTS

Tales From an Ex-Husband
Copyright © 2019 by Harry Carpenter.

For information contact :
https://www.facebook.com/Hcarpenterwriter
www.hcarpenterwriter.com

ISBN: 978-1794641662

First Edition: January 2019

10 9 8 7 6 5 4 3 2 1

This book is dedicated to anyone who struggles with an abusive partner, whether it be mental, emotional, or physical. Do not be afraid to speak up. Plan your way out, and make it happen.

I also dedicate it to the men and women of the Armed Forces, who deal with this type of stuff on a daily basis. May you conquer your Jody's and move on to a better future. Thanks to those in my old unit who went along for the ride with this crazy ordeal.

Also, my wonderful wife. I couldn't have been where I am today without her. She holds me together, and I don't think she realizes what a relief it is to know she will never be this crazy. I thank her for standing by me and I love her more than she will know.

I also dedicate to the following Fallen Soldiers; SPC Stanley Sokolowski, and my cousin, SSG James Carpenter. They took their lives, and in part, due to toxic relationships. I miss those guys to this day.

And finally, my last dedication, I promise. David Ward. Dude, I didn't even get into the meat of these stories. You were so intrigued to hear the stories of my troubled past with my ex-wife, and every time I finished a small story, it was always followed by a "bloody hell, she seems a right bit mad, didn't she?" I only wish you were still with us to read this book or have a beer with me and hear all about it.

PREFACE

Everything you are about to read happened as I experienced it. Nothing is fluffed, exaggerated or made up, crazy as they seem, because trust me, I was there. I've written it in such a way it is broken up into milestones in my life, so chapters may be longer than others. I've had this discussion with numerous people, to explain stories about my Ex-Wife in detail, only to have them dismissed as fake. But then something wonderful comes along; a childhood friend, or an acquaintance from the dark times of my past, who corroborates my tales, and helps cement the whirlwind of shit which was my life.

What comes as a surprise is how much of an idiot I was. The saying is, hindsight is 20/20, but I must have been blinder than Stevie Wonder wearing a blindfold in a pitch-black room and getting worse by the minute. We had a long relationship, all things considered. We began as high school sweethearts, and things were going perfectly. Ok, so this is the part before it all went down the drain, but there were signs back then too. I just refused to listen to them, as most people do when they are in a relationship. I'm hoping that my experiences can shine a light on other people's personal experiences and show that you are ultimately not alone.

I'll be using nicknames, codenames, and abbreviations for

most people, you know, for safety and their identity. To those that know me personally, I'm sure you'll deduce exactly who is who, not a hard feat. To those of you whom I do not know, who didn't bear witness firsthand to the shenanigans and chaos that was my first real relationship, buckle up. This ride will be wild, that I can promise you. This relationship spanned high school, up through my mid to late 20s. It lasted 11 years too long now that I am looking back on it, but if these things didn't happen the way they did, I would not be where I am at today, that I can assure you.

What I can do now is tell you my side, my thoughts, and my feelings. What I can't tell you is what went on in the minds of others as they judged my actions or why they were absolutely batshit crazy. While this all may be from my perspective, there were so many others that witnessed these things happen, I'm confident this side, is as truthful as you'll hear. Allow me to take you through an 11-year long trip through misery, abuse, and some crazy stories that you'll never believe.

Fuck you for cheating on me. Fuck you for reducing it to the word cheating. As if this were a card game, and you sneaked a look at my hand. Who came up with the term cheating, anyway? A cheater, I imagine. Someone who thought liar was too harsh. Someone who thought devastator was too emotional. The same person who thought, oops, he'd gotten caught with his hand in the cookie jar. Fuck you. This isn't about slipping yourself an extra twenty dollars of Monopoly money. These are our lives. You went and broke our lives. You are so much worse than a cheater. You killed something. And you killed it when its back was turned.

—DAVID LEVITHAN

CHAPTER 1

In The Beginning, There Was Light

The year was 2000. A fine time it was, with the turn of the century and all. We had all just survived the Y2K bug, one of many apocalyptic moments to happen in my life. The music was epic, the movies were awesome, and everything was carefree. At least for a 15-year-old. Life was typical for me; no girlfriend, no job, no aspirations. I had girlfriends in the past, but those relationships tanked hard, and I suffered from severe low self-esteem from it. None of those relationships really lasted more than three months, and as you know in middle school, are never really that serious. It also didn't help I am completely oblivious to any woman that shows interest in me at all. Maybe I'm just too nice, or maybe I'm just an idiot when it comes to the other sex. In either case, relationships didn't just fall into my lap, nor could they be obtained by actually trying my hardest.

I had gone through my ninth-grade year hoping and wishing to get some sort of relationship. I asked out a friend I had made, this rocker chick who seemed cool, and she had me ask out some other dude for her. I asked a girl out from my Business Economics class but was shot down faster than a plane in a no-fly zone. This started to feel like the story of my life. I didn't let that get me down, so of course, I tried again in biology with a girl I had a crush on, again, the same result. I survived the ninth grade, barely, but I made a few friends and kept chugging along. The summer was uneventful as well, except for the fact my parents went through a divorce. I didn't really talk to my dad for easily the next four to five years. That whole ordeal was pretty impactful on my high school time, overall. Tenth grade began again in September, and I was already over being at school.

One of my middle school friends, Breezy, decided he wanted to go to my school. He transferred in the tenth grade, which made school a bit more bearable. I had a math class with this red-haired girl, not to be confused with Charlie Brown's love interest. We made decent friends and chatted often during class. Somehow along the lines, she met Breezy, and he started dating this red-haired girl, shortly after he joined me in high school. She was odd, had a strange obsession with Backstreet Boys and Tim McGraw, but otherwise was ok people by me. She lived toward my direction home, so we would ride the mass transit systems together. She was the ignition to this dumpster fire that followed.

One day in the hallway of the school, she approached me to let me know I had an admirer. I assumed they must be blind, because who would date a kid who was severely underweight, wearing cartoon character shirts, and sporting a bowl cut style hairdo. I wasn't much of a catch, which I tell myself all the time even to this day. As you could imagine, this came as a shock to me, to have an admirer, how absurd. But, of course, I played along with this little game. She showed me a few pictures of this girl, she wasn't bad looking, actually kind of cute. She didn't look like she belonged under a bridge threatening goats for gold or something, so that was a plus.

Of course, I opted in and said to tell her friend to meet up with me. She told me to meet her in front of the health class they had together after the next period. We, of course, met up in front of her class, where she rushed past me, head down, holding her backpack straps and said "hi" as she passed a note. See, notes were all the rage before texting, tweeting, wall posting, or whatever the kids are into these days. We always took pride in folding them all crazy and complex, but I digress.

I read the note in my next class. It was something to the effect of "Hey, you're cute, my name is blah blah blah, and I like this that and the other thing." You know, the introductory format for that first note. Well, I responded, and before you knew it, we were dating. She seemed pretty normal, a chubby little Italian gal, but ok nonetheless as nothing apparent was off, or out of place. She too liked the Backstreet Boys and was obsessed with boy bands, which was apparent in all her notes she wrote to me. She would include nonstop lyrics from these guys to express her feelings, and I would, in turn, write her lyrics to the Smashing Pumpkins songs, seeing as they were my favorite band. I was very excited for myself, and my day of victory since I was confirmed to have landed a girlfriend.

I went home and told my mom. I told everyone who would listen to me. I was extremely ecstatic about my new-found relationship. A few days into the relationship, I got to meet her Grandmother one day as she got picked up from school. She seemed nice. Her grandmother seemed like one of those cool grandmothers, who spoil their grandkids and seemed pretty typical. She even offered me a ride to my bus stop early in the relationship. We made very small talk on the way, but again, my original decision stands. They were pretty cool people.

A few weeks went by, and I was offered to meet her family. I told my mom, and she gave the ok, and I went well out of the way to meet these people. I lived almost 40 minutes away, which translated to almost 2 hours by bus. I hopped on the mass transit and headed across town. Owning a car would have been a game changer, but I didn't drive until I was 24, which we will get into that piece a bit more in detail later. She lived in the north part of the city, and I lived in the southern part, down in the hood.

When I got off the bus stop, I walked to her street. She came out to greet me and took me to her home. I went into this really nice house, old Victorian looking Mansion far as I was concerned, coming from my little row home in Brooklyn. Inside the home, were five floors of "apartments". Each level able to be segregated off into an individual residence, complete with showers, bathrooms, kitchens, the whole nine yards. It was pretty kickass, clearly a place you could get lost in as far as I was concerned.

She had a large family, being Italian, but in terms of the immediate family she had a pretty standard setup; a mom, a dad, and a younger brother. She also had two dogs, both were massive; a German Shepherd and I believe a Rottweiler was the other. I was always a little dog and cat person so that was a big change for me. I had dinner with the family, we talked and got to know each other, and everyone seemed cool.

Her mom was a huge smoker. She wore jeans, t-shirts and trucker hats. Looking back, she reminds me of Charlize Theron's portrayal of Aileen Wuornos in that movie "Monster." her brother was average. Just kind of a goofy kid trying to find his place and wanting to share stories and constantly bug me with little brother stuff. Dad was a weightlifting Metallica loving dude, always sporting bandannas and Tie Dye Shirts. He seemed like a pretty chill dude, from what I could initially tell. Not a bad setup, given what I'm seeing here on the initial meeting. I'm getting into something good it seems.

Her parents drove me home after dinner and the movie we watched, and I felt pretty good about everything. All things considered, she seemed cool, her family was alright, and I had good feelings. Her family seemed pretty happy and appeared to have it all together. Coming from a broken home, with a crazy brother who tried to kill me on a regular basis, this was a breath of fresh air. Or so I thought.

CHAPTER 2

I Can Work With This...

Things were going great for us in the beginning. We were dating for several months at this point. We exchanged notes constantly in school, talked for hours on the phone and all that good stuff that couples did. Other classmates will attest to the amount of "tonsil hockey" that went down on school grounds. I still shared a room with my brother upstairs, but thankfully, that changed. I moved to the basement and built my man cave. Band posters were hung everywhere cut from "Circus" magazine, a futon which was my relax and sleep spot, and best of all, it was my own private room. I even snagged the computer to put in my room, so I could dial in and play on the internet to my heart's content. What more could I want?

As things were going well for me, I figured it wouldn't be long before things changed. I had to get a job. My mom wanted money for rent now that I had my own place, in our basement. So, I got a job at McDonald's, which was my first foray into the working world. I had plenty of jobs beyond that, to include making pool sticks, construction, and a billion retail jobs, but this one stuck in my brain the hardest. I enjoyed the crew, making a ton of friends working there, and to be honest, the job was easy at most times. The downside is I had to hurry home to get to work. I would work evenings, until maybe 10 at night, which was a different world than playing video games all night. I'd still talk to my girlfriend on the phone after work, so it all still worked out, even with a big cut into personal time. The reason I mention this is because it plays a vital part in "escape route number one" that I didn't take.

Warning, the bit I tell next is a bit messed up. I only lead with this because it is very personal and still bothers me to think about this. I only tell this part of the story with the utmost care and concern for others who are part of this story. With that forewarning laid out, I say again, it's pretty messed up. Ok, you've had a paragraph to consider this. Also, this is how I got by in English class. This, and extremely lengthy and exhaustively detailed words. I thank you.

I was riding the bus with my friend Breezy and his ginger girlfriend, as I always did. This time was different as they were looking at me strangely. Something they muttered to each other, then looked back at me. Was something wrong? Did I forget to shave the two hairs that were growing in? What did I miss? So, I stopped guessing in my brain and asked. "What? What did I do?" They both looked at each other, then back at me. The most serious expression washed upon their faces. "Umm...well, it's about your girlfriend. She's not a virgin."

Oh. Ok. Isn't this an after-school special? Teach your kid it's not a dirty word and all that? But for whatever reason, they were more mortified than full of giggles. What was so serious that they were poker face about this? I started to get really concerned about everything, and my mind started to race, so I asked "Oh, so, what, she had sex with someone before the age of 14? What the hell!? Who does that?" The look on their face told me a different story. They clarified to me "No. She was raped." Holy. Shit. What?!

I warned you, now, that was the "trigger" but it's not the disgusting piece, I'll get to that shortly. Of course, I had to live with

10

this knowledge for seven lifetimes, also known as two weeks. This bothered me. I never was intimate with a girl, hell I was 15 and McLovin had a better shot than I did at getting laid. But rape is a whole new ordeal. How does someone bring this up in the discussion? How do you ask? Do you ask? Can you ask? A billion questions raced through my head. So, I worked up the nerve to speak, and I finally asked her.

She got quiet immediately. She said she didn't want to talk about it, but it constantly happens. Constantly happens? As in still happens? Jesus Christ, what is going on? So, I asked what was happening, because at this point, if it keeps happening, an ass needs to be kicked. Is it a classmate? A friend? She finally broke down and told me not to get mad, or do anything stupid. "It's my brother. He comes in when I'm asleep and touches me. He sticks his little thing in me and I just try to close my eyes until it's over."

Her brother was much younger. I think 8 at the time. Either way, this is really messed up. I sat and thought about it for a while. I thought about all this pretty hard. I asked why she didn't put a stop to it. She said her family would be upset if she did, and they would punish her. The room got still. Do you know that sound horror movies make when the bad guy is nearby, that loud bass filled whoosh? I'm pretty sure that was the sound going through my skull. The family would be upset? What the hell? I thought this family was decent and would be understanding and supportive.

I told her she needs to do something, anything. Tell a doctor, tell a nurse. Tell someone. This is not cool. As I'm moments from parting ways for the day to catch the bus, she says "I'm just used to it and ok with it. He's just exploring." I smiled, and we split to get on our separate buses. That last line sat with me and still does almost 20 years later. You should NOT be ok with the behavior or accepting this for the norm.

"I'm ok with it." I'm not a doctor. I'm not a psychologist. But you should never accept this as normal. I was not ok with it. For days, I told her to do something about it, and it happened again. He went creeping in and did it again. What happened next, I feel justified but remorseful at the same time. After hearing it happened again, I couldn't handle it.

I got on the phone, damn near midnight. She had her own phone line at her grandmother's house where she slept sometimes. Not sure why at the time, but I know now. Her line didn't go through. I called her main number. Her Grandma picked up. I told her I really needed to talk. She was not a happy camper. Groggily, I finally get my girlfriend on the line. I lay down exactly what I needed to say. "Look, I am behind you 100% if you just come forward with this thing about your brother. I am absolutely NOT ok that you're ok with it."

She got quiet. A small bit of time went by as I lay on my futon, waiting for a response. "It's fine. Don't make this a big deal. I'm not." Wait, what? No. This is not ok. I'm only 15, going on 16, but I know this isn't normal. I said that if she didn't plan to seek help, I'm out. She again reiterated she will do nothing because it's her brother. I did it. I ended the relationship. I broke up with her at 1 AM, over the phone, and hung up on her. The end.

CHAPTER 3

Moving On Up? Lateral Movement.

I went to bed that night heartbroken and disgusted. Mostly disgusted. The next day in school was an awkward one. Thank god we were a grade apart and didn't have a class together, or that would have been brutal. I eventually started to feel less anxiety about being in the halls as time went on. I went to work, as I always did that evening. I worked at McDonald's, which was attached to a Walmart. Inside the building was a food court, a hair salon, liquor store, and more. It was more like a mall than a Walmart.

While at work, I was told to get a haircut. I had a long mop on my head, and my manager, Jason, demanded I get my hippy haircut. He handed me twenty bucks and said to go next door to the salon. I went, smelling like French Fries and shame, with my long hair. When I got over there, the owner greeted me with a smile. A nice, heavyset blonde lady, who was always super nice. I said hi, as I did usually passing by to get restock supplies from the back storeroom. She said her daughter was my stylist today.

Her daughter was actually my age. Sixteen years old. Little did I know you had to be licensed and stuff to cut hair, but what did I know? Well, she was a nice redhead girl, very cute. I had a crush on her for a while and couldn't ever do more than a goofy wave. While she prepped my hair for cutting, we made small talk. She asked where I went to school and favorite bands, etc. Turns out, she was just pushed to make small talk by her mom, and mom was going to finish my haircut.

As mom finishes cutting all my hair off, she spins me around to the mirror and asks how I like it. Of course, I worked hard on my hair, I was in a band dammit. My hair went from cheek length to a mature, close and tight hairdo, spiked up. She then whirled me around and got her daughter's approval. "Cute," she said. Cute? Me, or just the hair? Her mom jumped in. "Do you want to see a movie with us on Saturday? I'll buy your ticket if you can make it." I absolutely agreed. I was delighted. I moved away from a crazy situation and moved onto bigger and better things. However, my life never works out for me, and you'll find out. Over and over.

We went to the movie, she even held my hand, and gave me a kiss on the cheek. Granted, I already had the first kiss a few years back, held hands with a girl before, but this was cool. Of course, my awkwardness kicks in. I can't remember what I said or did, but it set me back a few points. Her mom dropped me off, and we said goodbye. I came into the house to hear my mom tell me I had a missed call from.... her.

I don't know why I called back. Why did I have an obligation? No one made me. Maybe I'm a good person at heart and wanted to make sure everything was ok. So, I dialed her number, and she answered, sobbing. I already knew this was about to be an adventure.

"I told them. Are you happy?" I shouldn't be the one that's happy. Honestly, if you have something like this going on, you need to find the resources and the cojones to remove yourself from that situation. She continued. "My family is mad at me, my Dad hurt me, and my mom put a cigarette out on me and now I'm living at Grandmas forever. Also, the doctor told me I'm a diabetic!" What. The. Shit. Whose family does this? Seriously? And I suppose some good came from it, to find out about your beetus early.

I didn't know what to say or do. I offered my best wisdom of what my 16-year-old brains could cough up and did what I could over the phone. I told her "I'm glad you spoke up. You shouldn't have to deal with that." She cried harder. I felt bad, but I could only say "I'm here if you need someone to talk to." and closed out the phone call.

In the weeks that followed, I walked to work one day, while talking to the stylist girl on my fancy new cell phone. Nothing particular, just boyfriend/girlfriend chatter. We never made it official. I walked to Walmart and saw her on the way in. I told her how my ex-girlfriend called, and she did not seem pleased. A few days later, she was dating the cart boy from the Supermarket across the hall, and I blinked out of existence.

That evening, I made a phone call. I said I would take her back. She filled me in on everything I missed; Her parents tried to kill each other, her dad making her eat her own vomit when she stayed over a few nights ago because she got sick at dinner, the cops shot her German Shepherd dog responding to a domestic violence call, and she found out she is diabetic from seeing the doctor to spill about her brother. What a freight train in the face worth of information. I had to take her back. We will get a better life. We will sort this out and live happily ever after.

Cue the Morgan Freeman voice: "But they did not live happily ever after."

The story goes on.

CHAPTER 4

The Rest Of My High School Days

Things got crazy as time went on. At this point, I was in eleventh grade and we had dated over a year. In school, it was as if everything and everyone was out to get me. I recall one such instance in the school cafeteria, around Valentine's Day, my girlfriend and I were suspended. This is one of those times I stand behind that she and I did nothing wrong.

I was grabbed up by my ICP Hoodie by school police. Yes, an ICP Hoodie, those were dark times in my past. The officer grabbed me by the hood and threw me to the ground. I was bleeding a little bit, but she didn't care. Both of us were jacked up and drug down to the administration office. Our parents were called. Neither knew what was actually happening since we were all just sitting at a table talking to friends.

Once our respective guardians showed up, we discovered what had happened. Someone told the administration, or school police, that my girlfriend and I were having sex in the cafeteria, on one of the tables. I immediately defended both of us, in the only way I knew how; humor. "Wouldn't we have a crowd drawn? Wouldn't there be more excitement? Why were my pants up when you grabbed me?" My humor fell on deaf ears, even if it made absolute sense. We were both suspended for two weeks for fornicating on school property. I was still a virgin, but apparently not on paper any longer.

A slight tangent to take here. My high school experience was wrought with conflict and, to be frank, absolute and utter bullshit. My school was primarily a black school. No big deal, as I grew up in Brooklyn, just south of Baltimore, and I had a diverse number of friends. I was easily "one of four white dudes" in the school. I was in high school shortly after the infamous Columbine Massacre. As the white kid who dressed in dark colors, listened to metal and had long dark hair, I was a target.

The final two years of my high school experience were spent being spot frisked, slammed against lockers, bag checked, locker checked, and more. Teachers didn't even believe it until they finally witnessed it themselves. It caused my attendance to slip. I hated going to school. I was always worried about the next thing I'd be accused of. I explain this portion because to hear the next piece, you must understand the culture of the place I went to school.

During my senior year, I'd say around March, I was waiting at the bus stop with my girlfriend. We figured out that she could catch the bus, ride a few stops, and get off and catch her bus. It didn't really impede her route or add time. While waiting at the bus stop, 5 boys approached me. Big, grown ass men, to be more exact. Compared to me, they were huge, since I may have been 100 pounds on a good day with a pocket full of rocks.

The boys surrounded me. My girlfriend backed away a bit to a safe position. I was about to get into a fight. Not my first rodeo, and damn sure wasn't my last. We made some small talk and one of them attacked from behind. I was on the ground, but not down. I was grabbing them from the ground and managed to work my way into a backward somersault and stand on my feet. "What the hell is that? What is your problem??" Which I felt was my equivalent of "ARE YOU NOT ENTERTAINED??!!"

As I emerged, fairly unscathed from my two-minute beatdown, they scattered.

I made my way back to school. I found my biology teacher and explained what happened. I was a little banged up, visibly, with a busted lip among other things, but nothing too bad. She called my mother. My mom made it a point to not drive to this school at any costs, and with my Dad living in a different state, he sure as hell wasn't coming down. I was on my own. The day was Wednesday. I remember this because, after my bus ride home, I slept and skipped school on Thursday. I returned back to school on Friday and was called to the principal's office.

I'm sure after reading the last bit, you can already surmise how this played out. I went to the principal's office and was directed to the conference room. I walk in, and one of the guys who beat me down on Wednesday was there, with his parents. Also, in attendance were the two school police and a few administrative staff. I was asked to recap what happened the other day. I did, to the best of my recollection. Also, I noticed the guy had his hand in a cast. It was store-bought, probably from a Walgreens or something, but in a cast nonetheless. They made notice that I really didn't have injuries or any visible bruising. After I told my side of what happened, they turned to him.

Like any good story that is made up goes, it began with "Well. What had happened was." The next lines to sputter from his face blew my mind. "Yeah, so like, we was hitting him a lot, right, and I punched him in the head a lot and broke my pinky." Shut. The. Front. Door. Did he just admit to beating me into my next life? But of course, the support at this school was nonexistent, at least for me.

Don't worry, that whole thing ties into a bigger thing that I'll talk about among other things. So many things. But sometimes going into those tangents really adds to the nutty story as it unfolds. Expect more of those further along. Anyway, I had a rough go my Senior year of high school. School police, fights, and drama were part of my daily routine. It was near the end of the school year that I discovered the snooty little rich kid (one of the few white boys aside from me) paid those guys to kick my ass. Why would he do this, you may ask? Well, I'll tell you.

The answer is simple. He wanted to date my girlfriend. Any logical person would just ask someone out, or make lavish attempts to win love, but not this guy. I still hate him to this day. He just wanted to date my girlfriend. Hindsight, I should have turned her over and moved on with life, but we wouldn't have this great story to unfold over 11 years now, would we?

We round out my final days of school with some kid running up to my girlfriend and kissing her and taking off. I realized what happened and hit the road. I used to be a fast runner, a damn gazelle. I hunted him down for three blocks, tackled him and buried his face into the concrete. Small victories, you know? Well, the good news is, I eventually graduated, after snatching my diploma off of the file cabinet, which is a funny story all to itself, since they couldn't find my payments to student dues. Score one more for my school giving me even more grief on the way out the door.

CHAPTER 5

Graduation, Moving, and Adulting

After graduation, I had a rough go in my home life. That's for a separate book, I'm sure. Long story short, I ended up moving in with a friend of mine, the same friend, Breezy, who dated the girl who got me and my girlfriend together. A short-lived residency, as he drove me bonkers. I mean, this dude ate my snacks, food, and had zero respect for any of my stuff. He lost my Vanilla Ice cd. Yes, go ahead and laugh, but it's the principle of the thing. He also ate my mini wheat cereal and complained about how they tasted horrible the whole time. It was not going to be a long partnership. I ultimately moved in with my girlfriend, at her grandparents' house after that whole ordeal because I needed somewhere to go. This is where things went down the drain or rather circled for a while before plunging into darkness.

I moved what belongings I could and lived in a tiny bedroom with my girlfriend, doing what I could to integrate. She was still in school, being a year younger. I took up work at a McDonalds in her neighborhood to make money because I felt like it was all I knew. I was doing what I could to get money. I walked to work every day. I eventually brought up the subject of me going to driving school since she was currently taking driving lessons, making her way toward being able to drive.

Maryland is odd, they require schooling, learners permits and more. It all costs money. After bringing up the subject, she tells me I shouldn't worry about it because she can drive, and I don't ever have to go far.

This statement is what threw me for a loop for the next 6 years. Let me be clear: not having a car sucks. It limits where you go, where you work and what you do. Still, I managed, and I don't even know how looking back. Either way, no car, no driver's license, but I kept going. I eventually landed a better job at a CVS Pharmacy. I thought I was hot shit because I was making better money than I ever did at McDonald's. My girlfriend worked at the Blockbuster down the road. Unfortunately, Blockbuster is not a good career choice, as we all know how that turned out.

She eventually quit Blockbuster and started working at my CVS. This started a trend that eventually drove me nuts. I worked in the photo department. Not going to lie, that job was pretty neat. I learned to develop film, mess with settings, and how to be electrically shocked by disposable cameras. That sure was an epic job. She was hired on as a cashier. I met some awesome people while employed there and learned some fun things in the process of working there. I continued to walk to work for the length of my employment, as it wasn't that far to go. I got to listen to my music on the way, so I honestly didn't mind the journey. At some point, her uncle, who Frankenstein'd cars for fun, got her a white sedan. It wasn't great, but it drove. She was able to move onto a job further away, at a day spa, which was more in line with her high school education of Cosmetology.

Everything was going great as we got closer to springtime. Prom came and went, and I had no interest in being there. I didn't even go to mine. I ended up getting sick and had a massive headache at hers and bailed out early. There was some point when I started missing hanging out with my friends from across the bay. I started having them pick me up, and I'd crash for the night every few weekends. Little did I know, this opened up a window for more grimy shit to happen.

I reiterate a previous statement, nastiness will be unfolding. I never witnessed this myself, but she spoke so much about it, that it clearly has to be true. On nights I'd be working overnight shifts, or hanging with friends, she would be in bed, asleep. Late at night, her Grandfather would creep into the bedroom, and peek under the blankets. She slept naked. Now, I'm not sure what is neither here nor there, but that's pretty messed up if true. That means this creepiness transcends generations.

After she confided in me about all of this, we made the decision to gear up to move into our own place. It was the smart thing to do. The only person I respected in her whole family was her Great Grandmother, who was dubbed Noni, Italian from Grandma. She was from Italy and had to be in her 90s. She was nice, and the whole family just shit on her. During my time living there, I did all I could to help that woman. She did the laundry, dishes, cleaned, and just about everything in her physical ability. The problem is, at that age, she was becoming forgetful, unbalanced, and having health issues. But let me say, that lady was a trooper. The only thing I had doubts about moving out, was leaving Noni behind on her own. Then again, she endured them for so long, she will manage.

Now, don't think this time of my life was without conflict. Most of it had to do with her family. Her mom was constantly starting drama. Dad started drama. Her grandparents always said terrible things to each other, to me, to her, to Noni. They worshipped the ground her cousin walked on, and their daughter, her cousins' mother, the one who married the car guy. We had to get out. We looked in magazines for apartments all over. This was 2004 and the internet was still in its infancy. We finally found a spot. They were townhomes, and right across the street from Walmart, Home Depot, and a ton of places to eat. Looking at it on a map, we were in a good location. We went over and signed the lease by the end of 2004. We were adulting!

I had to leave my job at CVS because of the commute. The upside is she worked across the street in the same center as that Home Depot and Walmart, which was super convenient. Here's the thing about me. I move quick. I need a job, I'll get one. I used to work at Walmart, McDonald's, and an automotive Warehouse, among other things. I've done it all at this point. I applied to an Office Depot in the same complex, for a technology associate: I knew computers. I had this. The job was going to pay decent, with benefits, and it was walking distance for me. Life was going places. I got called for an interview.

I went in to be interviewed, and the interviewers were the store manager and the technology department manager. The store manager looked like Ross from Friends, while the other guy looked like Fred Durst's long lost brother. Immediately, the department manager starts grilling me on questions. I get through them, but for whatever reason, I get told I am not working technology. I will work in the office supply department. What? That's less pay, and I don't know a damn thing about pencils! But I accepted it and went home, proud.

This is where that slight snowball trying to teeter downhill became an incline, and started gaining speed, and fast. I told my girlfriend I was hired, and she didn't seem enthusiastic whatsoever. Who doesn't sound excited? Who acts like that? Luckily, I made a lot of good friends early on, and we made the best of the manual labor position I undertook. Months went by, and I learned a lot. I was progressing, and even got promoted to full time. On the other side of the house, my girlfriend was tired of her day spa job. She quit but luckily picked up a job at a beauty supply store next door. It's nice when things work out like that, right?

I still maintained hanging out with my childhood buds. Breezy, Miguel, Jose, and the sort. These guys. I had known two of them since Elementary School. We went way back, so of course, we hung out. Once in a while, my girlfriend would snap at me for hanging out with them. She would say petty things like "Oh, going to go hang out with your boyfriends? What are you? Gay? Why don't you go fuck each other and get it over with?" Honestly, those comments were childish, unnecessary, and just plain stupid. I apparently couldn't have guy friends without it being sexual? Is that it? I'd stay over only because there were tolls, easily an 8-dollar trip one way, and it was 30 to 40 minutes away. Made sense to me to save gas, time and some toll money.

As time went on at my job, I befriended a few people from work, some of which I'm still friends with to this day. These guys saw some of the crazy behavior first hand and were some of the first to warn me of the danger zone I was in. As with anyone in a relationship, you never listen. You have to find out for yourself, which is the only way you will ever commit to the biggest decision you'll make. I wasn't there. Not by a longshot.

One of my good friends I had made in the office supply profession, unfortunately, decided to seek employment elsewhere. This dude was a good dude, and we hung out quite a bit. He was the only one who wanted to celebrate my 21st birthday with me. We will call him M, for short. Well, M and I were pretty tight. Him leaving did allow me for one thing: I stopped screwing around at work, took life seriously, and worked my way to the Tech department. Mission accomplished. Again, home life, my girlfriend was unphased. It's always nice to have a supportive girlfriend, right?

Well, M started a position at a call center. That job took him to shifts ending around 10 or 11 pm, and sometimes later. He would come over, rattle the mail slot, and absolutely scare the soul out of my body. I'd let him in and we would hang out, watch TV, play PlayStation, or go out to the local bar and shoot pool. We got out much more than childhood friends, granted, I lived across the harbor from them, easily 20 minutes away.

On numerous nights of the week, M would be over, and we would be playing a game or whatever we did that night, and my girlfriend would come downstairs. The time would be around 9-10PM, and she was ready for bed apparently. We would be fairly quiet. But she would say the same thing every time: "Tell M he has to leave." Okay, sure, but he is standing right there. I'd even offer going out with M to get out of the house. "No. It is time for M to leave. Bed. Now. Tell M it is time for him to go home." Of course, my sarcasm kicks in, and I'd look him dead in the eyes and I'd say "Hey, tell him to go home." We would laugh about it, but my girlfriend was extremely displeased by these shenanigans. Ultimately, M would leave, but he would be back in a few days, and we would repeat the process.

A few more months went by, I celebrated my second year, now working selling computers and things I loved. I was doing quite a bit of work, learning how and what to sell. My girlfriend was working at that beauty supply store, until one fateful day. The story goes, from her side, is that the new girl did it. I believed her, obviously, I had no reason not to. I had to take her side.

One night, my girlfriend was closing the store. As she did on so many occasions, but with the new girl, whom she had sort of befriended. She didn't have a lot of friends, so whoever tolerated her she took to easily. She locked up, as normal, and went home. Nothing out of the ordinary. The next day, I found out she was fired. She came into my store to tell me all about it.

She told me that the night prior, there must have been a break in because she remembers locking the door. There is no sign of break-in whatsoever, the windows and door unaltered. In the evening, at some point between closing, and the store opening, the safe funds, several bottles of product, and the cash drawer money were gone. Between money and a load of missing product, the estimated total loss was a few grand. As a shift lead, she had the safe combo, and keys to the store. So how else did this all go down?

The new girl. My girlfriend spun the ultra-believable story of the new girl leaving a brick to prop open doors to get back in after they closed shop. I stood by her and supported the fact it couldn't be her. They went to court and decided that they couldn't tell who did what since the cameras weren't working. The new girl had a history of theft, so she was ultimately charged with a small offense. Looking back, knowing what I know now, it was clearly my girlfriend or a team job. I never saw the money or noticed a huge cash influx, but I was also an idiot. The end of this tale is she was fired for theft. Good news though, she got hired on at the Pet Store around the corner. Nothing but rainbows and awesome around here, jobs aplenty.

CHAPTER 6

Further Adulting And Other
Dumb Things

I found myself in an infinite loop of drama and bullshit from this point onward. Her family popped back into the picture a bit more. She was spending time with her Mom and Dad, separated as they were, she found time for each almost daily, in addition to her Grandparents. Her dad had a huge chip on his shoulder about me. Not sure what it was, but I felt like the whole family looked down upon me. I worked at an Office Supply Store selling computers. I wasn't making six figures, but at least I was paying bills and not getting fired for stealing.

She started working at the pet store. Here's the thing about this location: it was directly next door to where I worked. It is what it is, but it was just damn close. Her first two weeks in, she came over to tell me someone had left a box of kittens. It's how we ended up getting our cat named Turkey. Yes, a strange name for a cat. No, she wasn't found in November or anywhere near Thanksgiving. She just happened to look like a rotisserie chicken or turkey when she sat. The cat was cool and was one of the better things she contributed to the relationship.

She befriended some girl, who named herself "The Feline" while at the pet store. Well, at least she befriended a cat lady,

I guess. This girl didn't like me from the get-go. Not sure what I did or said. She was sort of attractive, nothing to run home to mother about, but she wasn't bad. The two of them became best of friends after a while. They were always hanging out at her place, or our place, and at any odd hours. The two of them would play the "Tell M he has to go home" game. I haven't the slightest idea how that even works, in hindsight. She also didn't like M.

Now, Feline was one of those people who was that quiet bad influence. You know the type: they seem quiet and innocent, but deep down they are dirty, twisted, and manipulative. This girl ended up being this way. I get all this info out of the way to set up the next scenes that begin to unfold. Stay tuned kids, you're in for a wild ride.

One particular day, I was due for a phone upgrade. I asked my girlfriend to go with me, on account I didn't want to buy stupid things and wanted to be kept in check. She agreed, and since we both got off work at the same time, we walked over to the phone store. I must have killed damn near two hours in the store, looking at every make and model. Remember, this was the mid-2000s, there weren't many options to choose from, but I still wanted to get the right one. I eventually settled on a phone and promptly checked out. Happy with my new purchase, we started to walk home to the apartment, conveniently located across the street from this shopping center. The weather took a turn for the worse, and it was pouring. The wind was blowing so hard, it was raining every direction. We made our way past Sam's Club, and a cart struck me. We went inside to tell them, so I could maybe get some ice. Between the wind and the hill, the cart had such a strong force that it knocked me flat on my ass. We went inside to tell them so that I might be able to get some ice or something for my bruised ass.

After leaving Sam's we kept heading toward the apartment,

making our way down the small hill, across the street. We lived about three streets into the complex. We made our way to the street and then to the apartment. I stuck my key in and opened the door. What I saw next I still can't believe to this day. How could something so bad happen to me? I immediately closed the door and told my girlfriend to not look. She burst past me to see what I was talking about. She immediately began crying. The entire structure of the roof and second floor were now on the first floor. I could see the sky from the kitchen. We were devastated.

My first thoughts were to save the cat. By this time, the fire department showed up and told me to not go into the house for a pet. I told him to kiss my ass and went in. This was my baby at this point. Me and this cat got along so well. She would always choose to lay on me. She would nap on me any chance she got and enjoyed playing with her toys with me. I had to look for this cat. I ran through the house, trying to look under rubble, and moving anything I could while calling for her.

I finally moved a piece of sheetrock and debris from an end table, and she was there, curled up under the table, protected from all of the falling house debris. I found her cat carrier in the closet and took her to safety. The cat was ok. So, this wasn't so bad after all, everyone lived. I called the apartment office, who said they would deal with it tomorrow since it was after hours. Well, that's good customer service for you. My girlfriend called her grandmother, and she got us and away we went full circle.

It was a quiet ride, aside from the standard questions asking us if we are ok and about what happened. My girlfriend didn't say much to me the whole way there. We unloaded from the minivan and went upstairs to my girlfriend's old bedroom. Once the door closed, I asked her what her issue was. I know we BOTH just went through all of that, but why the attitude towards me? She just responded "If you didn't take so long getting your goddamn phone, we could have been home. I'm tired and cranky and just want to sleep." Seriously? Your only concern was to go to sleep? I flat out told her "If not for my phone shopping, you'd be dead. The cat too. You would have been in the bed, and ended up downstairs, covered in roof." She just glared at me. God forbid I buy a phone and save our lives.

The night at her grandmother's place was tense. My girlfriend didn't talk to me, and I didn't feel like talking to her. Sleep, or what we had of it, went by, and I had to call work first thing in the morning and let them know what happened. Her grandmother was dragging her feet about taking us back to the apartment but eventually did. These are moments, in hindsight, I really would have liked to be able to drive. When we arrived at the apartment, there were firefighters, police, and what I assume were claims adjusters for the apartments all over. We were not the only victims of the roofing but by far the worst.

After speaking to the rental office, they said they'll just move us into a new apartment and waive the set-up fees. Waive the fees? We better have a few months free of rent! Ultimately, they waived the current month of rent, and gave us a waiver on setup fees, since it was an act of God, because you know, God put the roof up. We took that for what it was and got keys to our new place. It was the same shape, size, and design, except the patio opened to a giant field instead, so minor improvements I suppose.

I spent the next three days, with coworkers and friends trying to move all our remaining salvageable belongings to the new place. My girlfriend? She was busy hanging out with Feline and partying or whatever. They were constantly shopping and eating out. Maybe she just needed retail therapy, and that's how she copes with what is going on. I needed everything back to normal. We had to get a lot of new furniture, and luckily one of my managers had an old couch he could offer up, considering the two we owned were crushed and full of water. Oddly enough, to this day, I still have the couch. It's salmon pink, but it's built strong. Can't beat old furniture.

Eventually, we got back on track. Things started to get back to normal. But my girlfriend always acted a little strange after that. Maybe she acted differently, maybe I noticed things more. Either way, all that time with her friend seemed to be doing more harm than good. I went back to work, and so did she. Weeks went by, and it felt like things were back on track, yet again.

We had been dating for about 7 years now. After that amount of time, obviously, the next step was coming. I proposed. I had to put a ring on layaway, but it worked out. I was proud of myself, I was adulting like a champ. We were to be married in the summer, in August. Her mentality shifted, and she didn't seem as angry at me anymore, so that was a relief. So, planning the wedding had begun.

I'm a planner by trade, and I like to have control of things. It's just my nature. I like to be the one to drive, be player one in video games if I select game options, there's not a lot I relinquish control on. It's an issue of mine, and I'm well aware of it. So, planning the wedding fell into my hands. We started looking for venues, DJ's, catering, the works. One day, she comes home and says "We are Baptist now and will be getting married by my new pastor in a church. Our church. In front of God and all of my family." Wait, what? Where is this coming from? We ain't religious.

As it turns out, she drove over with an aunt of hers to become a member of a Baptist church. I'm not sure what you do, sign a form, raise a hand, sacrifice a chicken, but whatever it was, she found a new religion, from Catholic to Baptist. Don't ask me the difference, because I couldn't tell you. Yet here we were, members of a church. She dragged me out to one of the evening mass ceremony things where we sang about Jesus and his friends. It was interesting, to say the least. Afterward, she took me to meet the pastor because he had to evaluate our relationships and us as individuals before he would marry us.

I wasn't aware it was his decision, but I was told he needed approval from God, plus my girlfriend said it was the right thing to do. So, he questioned us and prodded, and ultimately, in the end, deemed us worthy in the eyes of God to be married. Fun note, I myself am ordained, and anybody with 50 bucks and a valid marriage license is worthy in my eyes. I never knew people went through all of this to get married. I was assured that it was entirely normal. I didn't know any better anyhow, so I went along for the ride.

We now had our church, our pastor, and it seemed like we had most things under control. The pastor said we could have our reception in the basement area, which was kinda cool. A one-stop shop, we do the thing upstairs and head downstairs to get loose. Then the pastor says something that didn't sit well with me. "You may have the reception in the lower level, but there is no air conditioning, and we do not allow alcoholic beverages or music of any kind to be played. Is this understood?" Understood. I understand you guys really know how to party. I decided it was time to find a reception venue.

At this point, nothing has really gotten too crazy for me in terms of this relationship. Sure, she was controlling, manipulating and pretty much just a grump to be around, but it wasn't all that bad, right? I proposed the idea that since I was working full time, and making reasonably ok money, that I go to driving school and get this little process started. Once again, as before, she said it would be better if I put the money toward other things. After all, she did have the car and said she would take me where I needed to go, if anywhere.

The springtime came, and I went out with a friend to a five-day outdoor camping excursion, for none other than ICP. Yes, the clown guys. I know what you're thinking, and judge me all you want. We went out on this trip, this being my second one, looking to have fun. My fiancée seemed cool with having me out of the house, so I took my vacation and my buddy and I packed the truck and hit the road. We drove to Ohio, and stayed for a few nights in the woods, drinking, listening to music, partying and hanging out with interesting characters.

On the final day, my fiancée called my phone. She said I absolutely needed to come home, her uncle passed away and she is not in a good place. I told her we would be back the next morning, since it was after 8 pm as it were, and driving a few hours after being up all day doesn't seem like a good idea. She cried. She pleaded with me. So, I asked my buddy to leave early if possible. He agreed, but we watched the headliners perform, and we then hit the road, destined for Maryland. As we were driving along the road, a massive rainstorm hit us, it was pretty awful all things considered, and with a lack of sleep, and nasty weather, we were looking at pulling over for a bit. We must have been at the PA state line when she called my phone once again, now screaming at me to get home. I told her we were on our way as best as we can be.

Clearly, this wasn't good enough and she started shrieking loudly to get home immediately. My buddy grabbed the phone and proceeded to curse her out and said he isn't trying to die to get home earlier. We pulled over and he rested his eyes for twenty minutes and we tried to let the storm pass as best as we could. I turned off my phone after the third call from her, at 2 am. The rest of the drive back was interesting, and once the storm cleared, was a little easier to manage. We did have to pull over a few more times, for bathroom breaks and to wake back up.

We arrived at the apartment around 7 am, and my fiancée

was nowhere to be found. I assumed she was with her family, so we unloaded the truck of my belongings, and I asked for a lift to her Grandmother's house. They hadn't seen her and didn't seem too beat up about a dead relative, and not a single person mentioned it. I thought that was odd, so I decided to bring it up. They had no idea what I was talking about. My buddy was pretty pissed that we drove a few hours across two states in the pouring rain in the middle of the night for someone who didn't exist.

He drove me back to the apartment, and there she was, hanging out with her little friend, laughing and joking and having a good old time. I immediately interrupted and asked, "How are you doing?" they both looked at me and started laughing and carrying on again. My buddy lost it. "I drove this fucking truck from fucking Ohio in the fucking rain for a dead fucking uncle and you don't even give a fuck??! Fuck!" he was livid, to say the least. We so poorly packed the tent up in a hurry it ended up getting broken, so now it was trash. And all for what, exactly?

CHAPTER 7

Wedding Bells Are Ringing

We finally get to the middle of this story. Realistically, it's just the midpoint of the relationship far from the middle of the actual tale I'm presenting you with. After all of this craziness, we are still rolling through with everything. My friends and family were told about the wedding. Word went around to coworkers. We were headed down the aisle in a few short months, and it was crunch time. Time to plan, save money to pay for things, and get this show on the road.

My fiancée was fired from the pet store not long after being hired. She may have been there 4 months or so, I can't recall. But she was fired, nonetheless. I wasn't initially told what for, but it must have been serious. She spent her lunches at my store already, and all of her days off were spent hanging at my store. Once she had a ton of free time, the obvious next step was being at the store daily, for hours at a time. Yay me, right?

Apparently, manager Fred Durst took a liking to her, and offered her a cashier job, on the spot. And just like that, we were coworkers again. In a way, it worked out. I'm extremely competitive in an environment where success is rewarded. We played off each other very well, and we competed heavily to sell the most extended warranty plans. The store's numbers were at an all-time high. She was doing great and probably found her calling. That's when it came out. All of the dirt spilled over for the world to know.

One of her old coworkers happened to approach me while buying pet food for my cat. She asked if my fiancée really got hired at Depot with me. I nodded. "Wow. You do know she got fired, right?" I nodded again, well aware she was let go. "Yeah, they caught her stealing from the register and the manager fired her right away." Wait, what? She did what now? Well, that's interesting. She went on to tell me how this manager had it out for her, and so on. So, who's to be believed? Well, obviously my fiancée was in this boat before, so, what to do?

I didn't say anything. She had to pay her half of the rent too and if she got breezed through the system so quickly, so be it. She seemed to be doing great at this place, I'll just ignore what I heard. We began discussing wedding plans, like colors, songs, DJ's, and more. We managed to settle on a few items, such as our DJ, who was a family member that also worked at a local radio station. I thought that was pretty epic. We decided on the colors, of red and black, Wolfpac in the house for those wrestling fans. After red and black were selected, her aunt said our wedding colors were purple, green, and yellow now. What? Like a rotten grapevine?

I was not cool with some of these things but felt powerless to change anything back to my wants. I did, however, find a solid loophole called "I do what I want." It's a decent loophole, where my best man and crew still wear red and black. I opted for cream color for the groomsmen to differentiate between each of the roles. I asked Breezy, my brother, and one of my good friends from Office Depot to be by my side. All agreed and were all in for the ride. At least a few things were manageable. We moved onto catering next, which I thought would be an easy feat. I stand corrected to this day because her family got involved.

Catering selection should be fun, and all about taste tests. However, with my fiancée, I got none of that excitement. Instead, I was told we weren't wasting our time and money seeing these places for food and that her family would prepare all the food. Okay, I suppose that also works. Strike one for my side, we are not picking the food. I still had music, right? Honestly, at least her cousin was good people because he knew how to play wedding music and had decent taste in tunes. He also wasn't swayed by the controlling decisions of everyone to play top 40 oldies hits and Backstreet Boys.

We still needed to find a venue to host the reception. Thankfully, my window-shopping method of staring out the window looking for something as we drove around paid off. We found this little place, really close by her grandparents' place. We went in, and the ballrooms were pretty decent. Mirrors on all the walls, chandeliers, hardwood floors, it was pretty solid. We immediately started to price it. Twenty-seven thousand bucks. Wowie wee woo, what are those numbers? That's a lot for a room, but after all, it is a wedding and these things aren't cheap. So, we put the deposit down and were told the balance needed to be paid two weeks to the day of the event. No problemo, now that everything is out of the way.

We had a surprise small bridal shower in the basement of the church. I figured, why waste such a good space? I told my bride to be that we needed to go up to the church because they were having an issue. She called her family to verify and her Grandmother played along. So, she picked me up from work, and we headed up. We arrived to see a decent turnout, which was very awesome. They decorated it and we had friends and family turn out, even my mom, brother, and Grandma, which was a hike for them. We partied, and I was grabbing pictures of the festivities. I came up to Feline and went to snap a photo. She immediately struck a pose and said "Being a model, I usually charge for my photo. Consider it your wedding gift." Did I mention I hate this chick?

We creep closer to the wedding day, and everything is going smooth. Sometime in mid-July, I get a phone call from the reception hall. "Hello, I want to apologize to you sir, but we accidentally just booked your room for your wedding day. Can you cancel your event?" What? What do you mean "accidentally booked it?" I headed right down to get to the bottom of it with my fiancée. We were absolutely furious. The manager came out to speak to us, thankfully.

The manager said our room was booked, and there is nothing they can do about it. I had a few ideas, like tell the other people to piss off, we were here first. You guys don't check the calendar before booking? This is outrageous! They did luckily have a backup plan for us. They offered us the other ballroom, at no additional cost. It was much larger, and frankly would be overkill for the guest list we were having, but an upgrade is an upgrade. We finished paying the bill in full. They told us my favorite part: We cannot set up until after 11 AM the day of. The wedding was at 1 PM. Are you kidding me?!

The week of the wedding was madness. I was trying to get everything I could complete at work. My main goal was to make department manager since Durst got canned for stealing from the safe. They brought in some filler manager, he seemed like an ok guy, but initially, I was upset they didn't just give me the spot. I worked my butt off making sales, and overall improving the whole department. At home, I was making sure we all had our tuxedos, floral stuff, and all of the last-minute checks.

We were only a few days away from the wedding and heading home from the church late one night. We were sitting at a red light at a three-way intersection, and some asshole turned and kept turning. He smashed the entire driver's side of the car in, bounced off our car, hit a light pole on the opposite side, and hit another car three or four behind us and drove off. I rescued my bride to be from being pinned in the car, she was fine thank god. The damage to the car was outrageous. There was a bunch of purple looking car paint streaked down her white Mazda. The entire front wheel well caved in. It was a disaster.

The cops showed up and asked for our license and registration. The car was registered to her grandfather, and we explained that. Now, I've never had good run-ins with the cops in my past, but I knew we were ok here. She was too upset to talk, bleeding and shaking, so I filled in. "Sir, you need to step back. Is this your vehicle?" "No", I said, "I was the passenger. She is in no shape to talk to you and I'm fairly level headed." They cuffed me. This upset her more. The guy in the car behind me got out and shouted at the cops to leave me alone and stop wasting time on whatever this was, and go find the asshole in the car. Apparently, this guy got plate numbers, make and model, and even a description of the driver. What a model citizen. They did track the car down and he admitted to being intoxicated. Well, no shit, I could have told you that. Ultimately, he didn't have to pay for any damages, and we were forced to retire the car to her uncle so he could fix it up. We went home, shaken, trying to focus on the wedding.

Luckily, I have awesome friends, who sometimes had awesome ideas. Breezy came up with a pretty killer idea. He suggested we go half on a limo, and the ladies can all ride in that, and we can just ride in his car. Feline, her aunt, and her cousin were her maid of honor and bridesmaids. That would be pretty killer to surprise them with a limo, so we booked it. A day or so later, Feline backed out. She said she was busy that day. Literally been planning this out for ages, and you decide now is a good time to back out? Thankfully, Breezy's girlfriend K subbed in, even got a dress in record time.

They were staying at our apartment and I stayed the night with Breezy. I just hoped he wouldn't drive me bonkers overnight. Tomorrow was the day. We woke up fairly early. I shaved, spiked my hair up, and threw on my tux. We headed across the tunnel, and up toward the church, making amazing time. I get a call from K, who said a big limo just pulled up. We giggled because our plan worked. They were pretty excited to get in a limo, but they wanted to make sure it was all good. The limo driver apparently needed payment, and I said to tell him we will pay him at the church once they get inside.

They get carted by limo, and we head up by car. We swung by the reception hall to start setup. Several of the guys got there to help also. We get inside, and the place is a mess! There is trash, tables everywhere, trash cans all over, an absolute disaster. We have two hours to clean and set up and make it to the church on time. We snapped into action. We immediately started rolling excess tables to the curtained storage area. The manager came in and asked what we were doing, that it was the staff's duty to clean and set up the room for us. The staff was not there, apparently.

I went off on the manager while moving tables and chairs around. We set up the head table, DJ table, enough guest tables, and the dance floor area. We also put up all of the food tables for catering. One of the guys even managed to throw down the floor buffer before we put everything together. We did everything down to Windex-ing the mirror walls. This is bullshit. I am paying damn near three grand for a dirty room and I am not happy.

After a long battle with the manager, they eventually started ignoring me. I didn't have the time to really dick around with them anymore either since time was tight. We cleaned up our trash, set the last few things up, applied table settings, and prepared to hit the road. My mom, brother, best man, and two other people hustled their hearts out. We hit the road, headed for the church.

I get a phone call from my fiancée saying to kill time, she wasn't ready for us to be there. Ok, sure, but shouldn't you be getting ready and all that bride stuff? We sat at a gas station around the corner for almost twenty minutes before getting the all clear. We took a few pictures using my camcorder, which was also the same device filming our wedding. We looked damn good. We finally got down the road and arrived at the church.

The limo guy must have been out to lunch, so we opted to pay him after the ceremony. We walked inside, and the place was full of eyesore flowers. Purple and green. Like a giant bruise. The tapestry was purple and green. Her aunt said it was what she wanted to do at her wedding. Sorry lady, if you didn't get the memo, this ain't your wedding. We pushed on, trying to make sure we had everything together. We had the rings. We had the camera set up. We were dressed to impress. Let's get this show on the road.

The ceremony itself went fine. Nothing crazy, no interruptions, no disasters. We did the thing, and it was over. As we were all leaving, Breezy rolled his ankle on the stairs. Luckily, we got him to the limo, and all was well. All of the bridal party crammed into the limo, and it was spectacular. We started heading down the road, and before you knew it, we were at the reception hall. We took the scenic route, I guess to ensure the guests got there and were situated before we were. We arrive outside and get out of the limo. The limo driver says we have to pay, but he can't find the credit card machine. He thinks he left it at my apartment when he picked up the ladies.

Ok, whatever dude, hit the bricks and I'll pay the invoice over the phone when I get home or something. Nope. He needed payment, immediately. That's not cool dude, I got a wedding to go to. He started getting an attitude with me and running his mouth. He then said it will cost to drive to my apartment because he left HIS machine there. Nope, not cool either. He started getting physical.

The great part about this, if my wedding photos are still floating around, there is a flipbook of me in the background, while the others took pictures outside. That flip book consists of me fighting the limo driver and being held back by two of my friends. It's a classic, and honestly one of the more memorable moments. We decided Breezy would ride to the apartment and get the machine. I gave him my key, and after we were all introduced as the bridal party, he went on an adventure.

Thankfully, we stalled for time with music and food. Her family made spaghetti and meatballs, ravioli, and salad. We really went all out with the catering. One of her relatives handled the cake too, it was pretty normal and meh, but we made it work. I went and mingled for a while and had great conversations with everyone. I invited my boss, coworkers, friends, and family. After much mingling and stalling, Breezy arrived. Boy, was he pissed off.

He explained to me that this asshole didn't leave it at the apartment, but at the church. I guess my wife didn't tell anyone they saw the card reader and snagged it. Our house was ten minutes away and the church was forty. Huge difference, and explains why there was such a long absence. He said he paid the whole damn thing, didn't tip and told the guy to kiss his ass. He also drove back in his car and sent the guy on his way. Rather than we ride in the limo back home, he was now gone. I had some words for the company next business day.

The reception was the best it could be, all things considered. The DJ was playing good tunes, and I even performed a song, dedicated to my new bride. My wedding gift from my store manager was a brand-new promotion! I was now a department manager, pay raise and all, effective immediately, to include my wedding vacation time. Of course, it wasn't all happy times and matrimonial fun. Shortly after a few toasts were made, my wife was pouting. No particular reason why, but she just became a grump. I carried on, and danced on the dance floor, and had a blast. She didn't have a daddy-daughter dance since her father was being petty and didn't show. They were starting the divorce process and he didn't want to be there. Her Mom showed, in ripped up jeans and a Budweiser shirt, but at least she was present. All in all, the wedding wasn't too bad of an event, even up against the odds it was against from the start. That clearly should have been a sign right there. I surely had enough of them.

CHAPTER 8

Post Wedding And The Decline Of Everything

What can I say? The absolute batshittery didn't really show itself until after we were married. Up until this point, there were some belittling's, verbal assaults, and we did have a few physical tussles. Most of the physical activity was me trying to either block and defend or push her away. I, to this day, have not laid a hand on her, and any injuries she received were due to her striking me, much like homeboy from high school with the weak pinkie.

The real fun began when her Dad got into the mix. This guy was super roided, extra aggro, and a ticking time bomb. I can't even begin to count the number of times he tried to corner me at work, home, or out somewhere to fight me, often times throwing punches. Cops were called, and he was clearly not afraid to go to jail, again. I was getting it from her family, as well as her, physically, and it was getting crazy. I really didn't know any better and pushed onward.

Even though I was a manager, and my wife was a lowly cashier in the same store, it worked. I managed to keep it absolutely professional, and management took notice. We were put on opposite shifts almost every workday, which helped. I managed the department pretty well and felt I was running the store pretty ok also. I considered myself to be the fun manager. I don't crack the whip, but I also expect work to be done. If you want to run to Dairy Queen on the clock, I didn't see nothing. Just make sure you come back with a milkshake for me, I can be bribed to look away. Morale was always decent on my shifts. Or so I felt. There was one particular individual who didn't feel this way, and she was upset she didn't get my position. More on that soon.

A few months went by, and I was doing great. We were driving sales at work, and I was training people on everything I knew. Then the happy time came to a halt. The register came up short, the third day this week, and we had only two suspected cashiers. There was a new girl, who came in late and seemed kind of shady. The other, none other than my wife. Mrs. "Fired From Two Previous Jobs For Probably Stealing." Since both previous issues were a "hearsay" situation, they weren't on her record apparently and no charges ever filed. I wanted to be sure we got the new girl pocketing the money, so overnight, we installed a security camera above the cash register from the ceiling.

Two or three days went by, and we had a few shifts worth of footage to review. Nothing useful, or interesting. Just a bunch of butt scratching and talking. Then it happened. I saw it go down. Money, going into a pocket rather than the cash drawer, and change from the drawer going back to the customer. The other manager and I reviewed the footage again and again. It was definitive, we had our man, rather, woman. We dialed the store manager and scheduled loss prevention to come in. Nobody steals on my watch.

The management squad reviewed the footage with the loss prevention manager, and it was unanimous. We all know what we saw. I was told to call the cashier in, and I did. I got on the walkie and paged my wife to approach the management office. She came back, after chatting with everyone and everything on the way, taking her sweet time to sashay to the office door slowly. She entered the office. I said my most dreaded words to come from management from my own lips. "Close the door and have a seat." The room was tense.

We reviewed the footage, and she was silent. She started to try to make excuses but couldn't find intelligible words to form a coherent story. I stood up and took a deep breath. "Listen. It's on video. It wasn't anyone else. That is your face. Your hands with customer money, and your pocket it goes into. If you were needing more money, you could have said something. As your husband, you could have said anything to me, on the clock or off. As your manager, you will be escorted to the breakroom to retrieve your belongings, and you are terminated, effective immediately. I'll see you at 7 when I get off work."

Her jaw dropped to the other hemisphere. My store manager actually gave me a look also. It's not that she wasn't going to fire her, it's that I went ahead and did. Who saw that coming, honestly? The office was quiet. She got up and left, with loss prevention shortly behind to help her out of the building. It was a dark time. Once everyone left, my store manager asked me why I did that. "Nobody steals on my shift. I don't play that. Time, product, or money. All three are a big no go in my book." I had previously fired a few employees for theft of product and punching in and disappearing for a while. If you're asking, no, there was no return milkshake for bribery, just went off somewhere and strolled back in hours later to punch out for lunch or shift. They knew the risk of not bringing me back a vanilla shake.

The walk home was quiet. Everything was going on in my brain. I must have played out a hundred scenarios in my mind of what was waiting for me behind the apartment door. I saw her car in front of the building, so clearly, she was home. I opened it up and closed the door quietly. She approached me with the biggest stank look you have ever seen. Her expression changed quickly, and she said, "I just got hired at Comcast today," and went upstairs. What the hell? Is she literally getting hired places like this, before the other job can document her sheistyness? How did she land a job so damn quick? I had questions.

A few days later, I found out from M that one of the former employees from my store went to work for Comcast after he walked out on his lunch break and never came back. I'm partially thankful, since that is what set in motion me getting to where I was, so I wasn't too mad in the long run. He and my wife were decent enough friends and apparently helped her land a job in there. Seemed like half my store went to work for the cable company.

She did reasonably ok, considering the next few months were training wheels phase. I kept doing my job, and she did hers, working crazy call center hours that I remember M having to work. On one evening, I was watching Half Baked on Cinemax, which is an epic movie. I must have fallen asleep at some point because my wife came through the door and walked into the living room. I was awoken by a loud gasp and a massive slap, and I didn't get the number to that bus.

I look over, and on the TV is some Skinemax special, Alien Vixens from Venus or something, with boobies and softcore porn going on everywhere. Firstly, I was that many years old when I learned dirty stuff was on that channel at night. Secondly, I was literally sound asleep when she came in, so some questions would have been nice. She hit me again. "You are disgusting. I can't believe you would watch this garbage. Is this what you want??" Yes. I want a green space alien chick with four boobs, you got me. She stormed upstairs, and this began the phase of withholding sex. I never did remember the name of that movie, nor have I seen it on the listings since.

It must have been about February or March when the drama

snowball started gaining momentum. I understand my friends are inappropriate, asinine, and goofy, but they aren't harmful or malicious. Let me say that her friend Feline was an absolute savage. The more the two of them hung out, the worse it became. This girl was a trip, and it's no wonder she came over to vent about all the guys she tries to date and how they leave her. She's bonkers, but I should have taken a page from those guys books and skedaddled. As I said, she was a bad influence on my wife, and pretty soon, she started dressing, talking. and acting completely different.

One on particular day in the middle of winter time, I came home from work as I always did. The two of them were home, and I figured I would just change clothes and go kill time at Walmart until this whole thing blew over and she left. Once I got in the door, they were both standing at the top of the stairs, holding a scrunched-up paper towel. "What is this?" It's a paper towel. "No, smartass. What is this doing in the trash can? Are you beating off at home when I'm out instead of fucking me?" The Feline chimed in also. "Wow. You don't even want to satisfy your wife, you'd rather jerk off to some slut online rather than have the real thing." Cornered and outnumbered, I was confused because I wasn't ready for this. I was in absolute shock.

I responded back to them with "Well, that isn't actually what you are going on about, its" and before I could finish, my wife took a big sniff of the rag. "No. I know what this is. This is cum. I'm sure of it." Well, like a good friend, Feline grabs a courtesy sniff, and I think she may have licked it. Cannot confirm or deny that piece. "No. It has to be. It smells weird." They both stood at the top of my stairs. Fuming while holding a supposed spoodge rag. I then had to tell them.

"Well, before I went to work, Turkey yakked on the hallway floor after eating her breakfast. I cleaned up the majority of it and flushed it. The last rag you hold in your mitts was what I used to go over the last bit to make sure I got it all up." Their faces dropped, and she threw the rag. "Oh my fucking God you are gross. We are leaving." They pushed past me and left for their night on the town. Ok, I'm gross, but I wasn't the one snorting cat barf from a rag. Hindsight, it was minor victories like that, they'd make me feel good. Strike one for me.

Another fun time with this lovely friend of hers: I was working quite a bit and happened to finally enjoy a day off. My wife wasn't due home until 5, so the day was mine and I knew just how to do it. I got a pint of Chocolate Chip Cookie Dough ice cream from the store, had some McDonalds on the way, walked back home, and removed pants. The door was locked, recliner kicked back, and I sat in my underwear eating ice cream. I was watching Armageddon at the time, which is still a classic.

Kicked back in my boxers and socks, I chowed down on amazing coldness while watching Bruce blow up a meteor when I heard keys in the door. I assumed my wife got home early, as the door opened. In walked her little buddy, Feline. She looked right at me, stared for a few, then sat on the pink couch. I didn't acknowledge her, really, nor did I ask if this movie was ok. I also didn't offer her ice cream. She sat there quietly for a few before she spoke up.

"So, she doesn't get home until 5? We were supposed to go out tonight." yup. Can't talk. Watching Bruce. More or less, I ignored her, because I really couldn't stand her. She kept trying to make small talk throughout the film until the movie ended. I went upstairs, took a shower, put on clothes, and was getting ready to hit the road to get out of the house. My wife came home a few moments later to find us both in the house. No questions asked, the two just went off somewhere together. "That was awkward", I thought to myself.

Later that evening, I was greeted by my wife who was being super pissed at me again for a mystery reason. I figured out what was wrong after she finally she calmed down enough. Apparently, I tried to seduce Feline! I went and took a shower, came downstairs in nothing but a towel, and tried to come onto her. Then I got some ice cream and played some sexy music on the boombox we had. I tried to feed her ice cream and put some on my chest to be sexy. Then I went and cleaned up after Feline refused enough and put on clothes and that was when she walked in the door. Man, that is a hell of a story to spin. I would never share my ice cream.

Time went on, and it must have been mid-March. It was before my birthday, that much I know. I had been a manager for quite a while now and felt I was still doing a good job. However, there was one employee who really wanted that position, and she figured out just how to do it. One particular day, I came into work and was immediately called to the manager's office. "Close the door and have a seat." Well, this can't be good. Apparently, legend has it, that last night when I was working the closing shift, I grabbed the store managers picture from the front of the store. I proceeded to pop holes in the eyes to see and made it into a mask. I then ran around the store, scaring the customers yelling "boogie boogie" or something lame. I immediately burst out laughing, which was clearly the opposite of what to do. I finally composed myself and said "Yeah, that's friggin hilarious, but I didn't do it. I'm all about shenanigans, but that's over the line, even for me." Apparently, she had made her mind up that I did it. I was ordered to turn in my keys, and I could not manage a shift alone anymore and I would require another manager on duty. I'd have no safe access, no combos, and everything was changed. A few days later, I decided to go into the management office and see a note that read "Don't trust him! Change the safe combo again and lock the file cabinets." Wow, talk about a punch in the face.

Speaking of a punch in the face, I made it through the shift and headed home. I went in, sat on the couch, and just cried. I had no control over what was happening. They believed some-one else because she was older and more mature, unlike my 23-year-old self. What a dumb kid, what did I know? My wife came traipsing into the room and knelt down in front of me as if to comfort me. "What happened? Are you ok?" She seemed to actu-ally be interested. So, I told her. I leaned back into the couch and let it all unfold. She looked at me as if to say something inspiring or motivational. "Wow. Feline was right, you are a little bitch," and grabbed me by the hair. I wasn't sure what her next move was, so I did the only thing I could do. I squeezed my knees into her gut and threw her to the ground with my legs. She got up and ran off out the door and into her car.

A few moments later, there was a knock at the door. I com-posed myself, and answered, only to be greeted by the police. This wasn't their first rodeo at this residence, with her dad pop-ping by for fisticuffs quite often. Yet, this was the first time she had called them on me. I explained to the officer what had hap-pened and that I used my knees to essentially take her down and toss her to the side, from a seated position. The cop asked me to turn around and put my hands behind my back. I was being ar-rested. They cuffed me and had me sit outside on the curb while questions were asked. I couldn't believe the types of questions they were asking! They said my wife had a black eye, bruised arm, scratches on her, and that I was in possession of drugs. They searched me and a bit of the apartment, found nothing. I told them exactly what happened, again. I went to the station.

A few hours later, the cops came to let me go. I never did find out why. Maybe I'm too dumb to ask the right questions, but I was free. I managed to get home after that ordeal. My wife was at home. She acted as if nothing had happened. Between the fight and arrest, it just really messed with my head. This was the start of a new trend with her. It may have been my first ride to the sta-tion because of her, but it damn sure wasn't my last.

I finally decided I needed to get my privilege back at my job. I was still on the payroll as a manager, and dammit I was going to do manager things. One late night, while eating at the IHOP, my wife told me that I was a loser and needed a real job. She needed someone stable with a real man's job. I needed to stop being such a pussy and actually do something. Her uncle was in the Army, and he can support his family. I needed to join the Army. She insisted this was the only thing that would make her secure. Well, my life couldn't get any worse at this point, so it wouldn't hurt to talk to a recruiter I suppose.

The next morning, she drove me to the recruiter's office. I met with the Sergeant inside, who seemed cool enough, as they all should, ss recruiters. We went over the basics. Random questions, and so on. My wife wouldn't shut up. She kept telling the recruiter I needed to do this. He reiterated that it was my decision, and he gets it. She got flustered at being dismissed so easily, and stormed out, apparently driving off. I talked to the recruiter straight, getting all of the facts. He did tell me that I would have to pass the height and weight requirements. Just looking at me, you could tell I wasn't passing weight.

We went to his scale to grab my weight, and the wall chart to get my height. He said how he's never had to do the opposite, usually, it's the big boys trying to slim down, not the other way around. We measured my height. Six-foot, one inch, or as I liked to always joke five foot thirteen. Next came the part I knew was going to go south, the weight. I stepped on the scale, and the bars leveled out around 116 lbs. I told you, I was a little dude. He sighed, and we went back to his desk. "Buddy, we gotta do something about the weight. It's not impossible, but with your height, you need to be at minimum a buck forty, but I got a plan."

The recruiter went on to explain that if I was able to scrunch my spine and neck a bit for the official weigh-in, the height may shave off an inch or two. He fished around for a short reference. It took him a bit until he finally came up with it. Operation Papa Smurf. "Smurfs are short, you be short." That's what he told me. If I dropped to 5'11", my minimum drops to 130, which ain't much better. But he can work with it. The bulking began. I drank protein shakes and did all I could while I was still working retail. One particular shift, the cat was out of the bag when the recruiters came to visit me at work. My boss found out I was leaving. I had no idea how to react to this. Was I in trouble? Would life be hell? Who knew?

Turns out, she was an Army brat herself and totally understood. I scheduled my visit for my official physical and turned in my two weeks at work. I managed to tack on almost ten pounds of weight, and it put me shy of 125lbs. I was pretty shy of my goal, but this weight was more manageable. The recruiter took me down to the Army MEPS station, and I went through my physical exams, blood drawings, and the whole nine yards. They didn't ding me on weight, which was nice to hear. I was about two days from my quitting time when I went to this examination. MEPS was basically the center for bringing new soldiers in. more or less, they check you out, make sure you're right, and put you on the bus.

In one of the rooms, they check your butthole, fun fact. Me and this other guy stood outside the door and spread the rumor that the guy sticks the fingers in your butt and he was a big Russian dude. You gotta have fun somehow. After going through the MEPS gauntlet, I made it to my last reviewer. The doc told me that I was denied entry. The reason being? He didn't like the way my scrotum looked. I honestly didn't know it was a ballbag beauty contest, or I would have steam pressed out the wrinkles. I asked him to clarify. He said, "There may be a possibility of testicular cancer." Wait, what?

I immediately booked a spot with a urologist pronto. By

immediately, I mean the first available appointment, in June. I quit my job on the exact day I was hired, which was pretty funny to me. I received my three years of service award, scooted out the door, and went off to go play soldier. I had zero ideas about how the hell I was going to make it with just a single income for a month or two. Finally, my appointment day arrived.

After getting my scrote an ultrasound and going through several "It's a boy" jokes, I was declared absolutely peachy. My ball had some extra fluid, which isn't a health hazard. It may pose as an annoyance, and they have surgery for that. I took the doctors findings back to my recruiter and we were off to MEPS once more. I was cleared and given an entry date of July 1st. Great, another few weeks to wait.

I was unemployed, but I made the best of the time I had left. I hung out with friends and even threw a going away party for myself. Friends and family attended, from both sides, even Feline. We partied and said our farewells. The day had come when I was going to ship off. I went down to the hotel with my recruiter that we had to stay at since we were up super early to eat and hit MEPS for final steps. He dropped me off, wished me luck and drove off. I checked into my room and thought about how to live the last day of my free life. I snuck out, hit Checkers and ate a burger and shake, came back, and watched some infestation show. The episode was a bird infestation with bird poop everywhere. My roommate came in, Big Willie, his name was. Chinstrap on his face muscled, and he seemed chill. He was equally amazed at this show, and we watched a few more episodes before trimming our epic facial hair and bedding down to start a new beginning.

CHAPTER 9

Army Training

T he next day, I woke up really early in the morning. I can't describe how early, but I never woke up before the world before. My roommate for the day and I got ready for the upcoming adventure and made our way downstairs. We had a continental breakfast for everyone that stayed. Apparently, this hotel was the place all new recruits began their journey from my hometown. We embarked on our journey to the MEPS station, where we were greeted by family, and friends to witness our swearing into the United States Army. Well, everyone but my wife was present, it seemed.

As it turns out, she didn't really feel like attending because it was just a waste of time and she will see the next one. News flash: there really isn't a second time. It's not like you graduate high school, only to walk across the stage again in a few months when it's more convenient. Alone as I was, I had already made a friend. Big Willie was a pretty chill dude, who grew up a few neighborhoods away from my childhood home. Small world. We made small talk until it was time to raise our right hand for the country.

The time came, and we were sworn into the United States Army. It was official, I was a soldier. I shipped off by bus, bound for Fort Jackson shortly after. The bus ride was decent, and I watched Ricky Bobby as what was to be my last movie for the next three months. I always enjoyed that movie, and it was nice to watch on the way down.

We arrived at the base, and the first couple of weeks were pretty uneventful. Being out of touch with the outside world, all you have to worry about is waking up before early and doing what you're told. We had access to our money, which is how we paid for haircuts and necessities like towels and soaps. One particular day, I tried to swipe my card to buy some supplies like soaps, and it was declined. I wasn't sure how, as this was the second of August, a day after payday. My drill sergeants were also concerned.

Luckily, the Army has made a few changes since what probably went down in basic training. I was allowed to call home to find out from my spouse what went down, how nice of them. I called my wife, and oddly enough, she picked up the phone. She sounded busy, but I needed to ask what happened, so I came right out with it. "I paid all of the damn bills, so we are broke until you get paid again. I had to ask my grandma for money, so you really embarrassed me." After that, she hung up. The drill sergeants made some jokes about this "Jody" or something taking my money, I wasn't in the loop.

Eventually, my money got back on track and I was doing much better off. The unit I was in failed to confiscate my personal bag, even at my personal request many times. This meant I had my books, MP3 Player, and best of all, cell phone. I managed to sneak off and call my parents, a few friends, and of course my wife. It really kept me in the loop with affairs back home I suppose, but at the same time, didn't really provide me any solid information on things either.

We were given phone privileges about two weeks before graduation, in order to help coordinate lodging arrangements and details. I offered my mother to come down, as well as my father. Neither of them took me up on the offer, but my grandmother stepped in to drive down with my wife to witness the ceremony. It was a solid drive down, but my grandmother made it many previous times since I had an uncle who lived 20 minutes from the base.

Graduation day came, and we were reunited with our families. My uncle ended up joining us for graduation, which was pretty cool. We were cut loose to be with families, and I knew exactly what I wanted. Burger King. They had the Home of the Whopper on one of our run routes, and smelling it almost killed us every time. We ate at the King, and it was everything I could ever want. My wife pouted that we could have eaten anywhere, somewhere fancy, not regular ass Burger King. You have no idea how Burger King tastes until you have been required to eat the same Army crap for ten weeks.

We were to part ways the following morning and set off to our job training, known as AIT, or Advanced Individual Training. Luckily, my wife brought me the items I requested: my Xbox 360, some games, my laptop, and a few other things. I was happy because I heard I would be able to use these things in AIT, and that was a huge game changer. I loaded my bags, and we headed to the airport on the Army bus. Fun fact, I had never flown before.

One of the guys I met in my unit, Chris, luckily was able to hang with me and get me through it. We were going to the same destination of Fort Huachuca, Arizona. I had never been further west than Ohio in my entire life, so I was about to see the world, one of the perks they told me of the Army. They weren't lying, they just didn't mention it wasn't any of the parts you wanted to see.

We arrived safely in Arizona, in a little town called Tucson. I never heard of this place, but then again, I didn't know much about the Wild West other than Tombstone, that Will Smith movie, and maybe Blazing Saddles. We stepped into the terminal, retrieved our bags and headed to the door. My first impression, it was pretty damn hot. And in the distance, wait, is that a cactus? Yep, it's official. I've landed in Wil E Coyote territory.

The trip to the base was about an hour or so through nothingness and sand, a complete change for a city boy like me. I had ridden through wooded areas, but this was a whole new can of worms. I had arrived at the base, and they stuck us in a room with 60 dudes to bunk in. A big open bay, bunk beds everywhere and a personal locker to store your crap. This was going to be an interesting change of pace from the 30 man bay we came from in basic.

I settled in and made new friends right away. My buddy Chris was the go-to, but I eventually branched out to others. There was an older guy, Rob, and a little guy named Dave, and a really tall guy also. These guys ended up becoming my drinking buddies at the bar, and we became awesome buds. I also made friends with classmates, once we got started with that. Overall, I really didn't have issues with anyone, and they were relatively great.

I would talk to my wife and other family members on a regular basis quite often over the phone. On one particular occasion, my wife decided she wanted to fly down to Arizona to see what it was all about. It was set that in mid-October, she was spending about a week down in Arizona with me. She said she would take care of all of the arrangements, like flight, hotel, and rental car. Cool beans, I couldn't wait. The day came, she hit her flight, and she was on her way, due in on a Friday around 1 PM.

We had night classes, so mostly my day was spent sleeping. In this particular case, I received a call around 10 from my wife, saying she would be in after 1, but she didn't have a rental car and would need a ride. Luckily my bunkmate, Kyle, had a few connections with other people and got permission to borrow a truck. I asked my instructor if I could go get my wife from the airport. Permission was granted. I just had to be back by the final formation at 5, after that, I was free for the weekend, until Sunday night class. Kyle and I hit the road to the airport.

A little more than halfway there, I got a call, and she said she is already at the airport. Well, that's much earlier than she said before, but whatever. She kept getting really nasty with me over the phone, telling us to hurry up and that she is tired of waiting. Kyle was getting his patience tested, given the fact the poor guy is as sleep deprived as me at this point. Once my wife called and hung up on me after yelling, he said he was about to turn the damn truck around and leave her ass there. Looking back, it sounded like the best idea in the world. About 20 minutes go by, and we arrived at the airport.

I texted her that we were there and asked where I could find her. She told me she was in a waiting area, waiting room C. I head inside, and started searching. I found A, B, and D. Where the hell was C? I kept going through and eventually stumbled upon C. Honestly, someone needs to learn the alphabet again, because those rooms were not in order. I walked through the area, scanning for my wife, looking back and forth, searching the whole room. She wasn't there.

I sent her another text, and said I was in C. Where the hell are you? I didn't get a response back, so I called her phone instead. "Where are you? You are wasting my time. I knew coming out here was a waste of time." I said to her "C. Like you told me." She got quiet for a moment, and said: "I said A. What are you, deaf?" Apparently, I'm blind too, because she sent that as a text message. She hung up, and I headed to A. She was there, looking pissed off as ever. I grabbed her bags and we headed to the truck. My buddy got out of the truck and did the polite thing to introduce himself. "Hi, I'm Kyle, Harry's roomie." She glared at him and said, "Don't care." To say it was a tense ride back is an understatement.

We got into Sierra Vista limits, and I asked where she was staying since that information was never disclosed to me. She looked around, and said, "Not sure, what do you got?" I literally have nothing. So, I used my phone, and called army lodging, since that was on post. They had a room available, but only for two nights. I booked it right away, and we headed there. Thank God one of us can do something right around here. Who flies down with no rental car and no booked hotel? Why lie to me and say you were square? She didn't work anymore since she got let go from Comcast for being a no-show, so it was my money anyway.

The week of that visit should have been fun. The first two days were the weekend, so I had plenty of spare time. since I didn't have a work call or have to be somewhere all the time. Our typical weekend routine was to hit one of the three or four bars, so nothing was going to change. I was fairly excited to take my lady to meet a lot of my crazy army buddies, so we made a day of it. We went to the local mall, which was such a sad disappointment, that she made note of constantly. It had a movie theater, a small food court, and maybe, at best, four stores. We spent most of the day looking at other places too, places I really loved, and still to this day think they were awesome stores. I loved the store Hastings, it had a little of everything and was pretty sweet out in the middle of nowhere. She hated it and complained that it was hot. Yeah, it's hot. It's Arizona.

Eventually, after much complaining and griping, we made our way to Buffalo Wild Wings to meet everyone. The gang got some nice seats outside on the patio, and it was mostly my classmates and friends out there. We got seated next to my drinking buddies, Rob, Dave, and crew. One of the girls, Katherine, happened to wave to me after she noticed me there. Just a friendly "Oh, hi classmate" wave, but it was apparently much more than that, so I was told. My wife immediately took the defensive and said "I hate that bitch. Who is she?" Wow, you don't even know this girls name, and you haven't even said two words, but you hate her. The table of girls came over, and Katherine said excitedly "Hey, you must be his wife! He talks about you all the time!" My wife immediately snapped "Oh yeah, sure, and who are you, his little Army girlfriend?" and got in her face. Part of me wanted to see some Army girls bury her into the concrete. The other part of me wanted to see that also. Really, this should go down, and I have no issue, nor will I step in to stop it. She asked for it.

Unfortunately, no altercation took place, but it was tense. She didn't like any of my Army buddies, which is a shame, because they were all pretty kickass dudes and dudettes. We moved on, and she wanted to go back to the lodging. The lodging was pretty nice, all things considered. It had all the amenities you would need, I suppose. She didn't want to do much of anything and was fairly grumpy the whole weekend. It was a real let down. The week came, and I had to go to class late at night, but I planned to spend my days with her and suffer from sleep deprivation if I had to. The first class night began on Sunday, so I told her once I got out of class, I'd come to get her, and we could sort out her further lodging needs. The class went from 6 pm until about 5 am, so I had some time to get back and power nap for a few. I managed to sleep until 9 after we did our physical fitness exercises. I called her, and she didn't answer. I decided to walk over to the lodging and see if I can wake her up, or whatever needed to be done. I went to her room, and room service was already up there, and the door was wide open, and my wife was nowhere to be found. I went to the front desk, and they told me she had checked out early in the morning around 8. Cool, now the fun part: finding where the hell she went.

I finally got a call from her about a half hour or so later. She said she was walking around on the base and doesn't know where she was. I asked her to describe it to me, and she said, "There are a bunch of Army buildings everywhere." Probably the best description I could get because I knew exactly where she was. I asked her to give me a street name, a building name, or anything that would tell me something more specific. She replied with "I don't know, they're all hard to pronounce." I made the walk all the time, being that I had no car, I was able to learn my way around, knowing street names, landmarks, and shops. She finally said she was coming up on a gas station. I knew exactly what she meant and where it was. The gas station was across from a giant parade field, which is what I asked her. "I don't even know what a parade field is so why the hell would you ask me that?" Wow. It's a field. Do you see a gas station with a lot of big fucking nothingness in front of it? She couldn't give me a straight answer still, but I made my way down there.

I arrived to see my wife inside, with all of her bags, sitting at the little dining area in the shoppette. Shoppettes were almost like little convenience stores, mini 7-11s or something. She said she was hungry and didn't know where to go eat. I told her there was literally a Burger King across the street, and she said she didn't see it. So now she was tired, hangry, and in a genuinely bad mood. I decided to ask why she hit the road so quickly and not even wait for me. She told me she couldn't wait that long. I'm still not sure why she was in such a hurry, or where she needed to be that she couldn't wait for me, on a military base, in a different state. Apparently, she booked a room for the next few nights at a Motel 6, you know, to keep it classy. I knew where this place was, the hotel parties always took place there, when the soldiers wanted to go out drinking but not at a bar. I called a transportation van to haul us out there. I dropped her off because after the navigation adventure, check in, and lunch, it was time for me to go to class. I set off for class and told her I'd be back the next day, and I'd call her on a break.

I went through my class, and the next two or three days fine. The lack of sleep was manageable, but I could have been better off sleeping, looking back. I made it a point to spend time with my wife while she was visiting. She came down to the living area, our sixty-man open bays where we were housed, one morning. She had all of her bags. I asked if she managed to get back on base or something, which would be nice, since I'd actually be able to sleep there, and no one would be the wiser. "Nope. I changed my flight and I have a cab to take me to the airport." With that, her cab took her away to the airport. She cut her visit short by several days, she was supposed to fly back on Sunday. I guess she was bored while out in a new state with plenty of things to look at. I always said, Sierra Vista is a great place to visit, but I wouldn't live there.

About a week went by, and she had been home, up to her usual things. I assumed hanging out with family and whatnot, considering she still didn't have a job. She did at some point pick up one of those candle selling pyramid scheme style jobs, but I never saw any of the money, nor did it go towards bills far as I could tell. She would always withdraw the cash and pay the bills at a bill pay center. This was still in the days of e-billing being in its infancy, so I never really saw the bills. One night, while at the bar with the usual crew, I get a text that reads "Guess what we're up to?" I don't know, and I hate guessing games. Planning to steal the Declaration of Independence or something? A few moments later, I received a barrage of photos to follow the text.

What I am greeted with is a flurry of photos, featuring her and Feline. The first two were selfies, being stupid. I don't even care. Thanks for sharing, right? The next one that followed was one of her kissing Feline. It was one that was half smiling, so it still looked like they were being goofy. One of the guys asked what I was looking at, and I said, "Just my wife blowing up my phone with pics of her kissing her friend." They stopped and asked to see. Now, this could have been perceived as wanting to gawk at the site of what was going down. They all immediately said "Bro, that is wrong. That's basically cheating on you." I dismissed that, saying they were just goofing around. And then more photos hit.

The next two or three were them in compromising poses and it got a lot lewder. I did not share those with the rest of the class. I thought about what they said, and technically yeah, she was cheating on me I guess. Or maybe she was just trying to mess with me. None of this type of stuff happened while I was home. There was no happy fun time three-way happening at all in my home with me in the middle. So, what is this even about? I drank a little heavier that night. I texted her late in the evening to ask what that was all about, and she only said "What, you don't want pics of us making out and stuff? Fine, no more for you. I figured you wouldn't like it anyway." What in the actual hell is going on with my life?

Another month went by, and it was nearing Thanksgiving. Some people were taking the four-day weekend to go home and visit family. I stayed behind as most did in order to save up for Christmas leave. On one occasion, speaking to my wife over the phone, the conversation came up about going to the ocean. She was going to take my brother, and he was supposedly paying for it. My brother is gay, so I'm not suspicious of anything there. What I was concerned about, was my brother is pretty much a loser and has no job and mooches off my mom. How is he affording to go to the ocean? Also, its November. Who goes to the ocean this time of year?

Turns out, it's super cheap to go to Ocean City this time of year. I mean, you learn something every day, and that made it more believable. So, they went, and I was fully aware of the trip.

Now, my brother is by far the least trustworthy person you'll ever meet, but there are moments when you know the truth and when he is bullshitting you. If he has any means of personal gain, he will spin you a tale, otherwise, he will tell it straight. I suppose that is a decent quality about him. You can filter out the garbage pretty quick in his stories. Shortly after the trip to the ocean, my mom called and said my brother had to talk to me. Now we don't talk much, and really don't talk at all these days, so this was odd for him. He got on the line. "So, it's about your, uh, wife. I got us a room, and four of us went up there."

Ok, so there was a party of four instead of two, which my wife denied to the bitter end. I had no reason to not believe him, so I told him to continue. My brother took his friend Sam, a girl, and my wife brought some dude along. I didn't know who, and my brother didn't disclose much. He said they slept in the same bed at night, but that was all he really saw. He thought it was pretty messed up, and had to tell me. One of the few times he was useful in his life, honestly. Now I had a billion questions. Any time I brought up Ocean City, she would dismiss it, or tell me her and my brother had a blast. She did mention Sam going along but made no mention of mystery date number 4.

I sprang to come home for Christmas. We got a decent amount of time to do so, but the clock started the day of. Flight time and any delays were all eating away at any precious vacation time I could spend at home. I flew in and landed at BWI Airport, which was quite a ride from our apartment. She did actually pick me up, and drove us back to the apartment, shocking I know. That's where happy vacation ended. She said she was hanging out with Feline and took off. Cool, you made plans for my first day home, alright. I decided to make the best of my time and see who wanted to hang out.

My first stop was my old job. See, when I was leaving for the Army, they all heckled me and said I wouldn't make it. Well, bitches, here I am. I walked in, said hi to everyone, and walked out after chatting for a bit. I was still limited to walking, so I went and checked out a bunch of stores. It was nice to be back in civilization, compared to the nothingness of vast open desert at all sides. After my exploration and shopping spree, I headed home. No friends really returned calls on the first day.

My wife got home around 6 or 7 at night. It was still reasonably early, and one friend, Todd, actually responded. We went to Buffalo Wild Wings, played catch up for a bit, then went our separate ways. My wife chatted with him, and I think the only reason she went is that they used to work together at Comcast. He was fairly in the middle for friendship, not my friend, not her friend, but right down the middle. We didn't have too many friends who were equally friends with both of us.

Two or three days went by and we had really done nothing. I got dragged out to a candle party meeting, where it was death by PowerPoint for six hours of my life. If I wanted this, I'd be doing training with the Army. I wanted to support her, so I went. I think I fell asleep in there at one point, fairly certain. On my first Thursday home, she had two candle parties scheduled, starting around 5. She had to go sell candles at two locations; her Aunt's house, and some lady's house. Both locations were reasonably nearby, no more than ten minutes or so away from our apartment. I told her I'd be fine and sent her on her way. I played my PlayStation, watched movies and stuff on TV, and did just about everything to occupy the time. Let me reiterate: having no car really sucked.

The time was now a quarter after ten. I got a little worried and called her phone. No answer. I waited another few minutes, the same result. I must have called her twenty times in the span of a half hour or so. The candle parties typically last an hour or two, so she should have been done by now. I thought her Aunt's party was the first, but I could be mistaken, and she is just hanging around and staying late. I decided, for safe measure, to call her family to see if she is still over there.

I called her Grandparents, and they said she was there to drop something off, but they haven't seen her since around 6. She didn't have any candle party, that was last week. What? So, she maybe had this other lady, and I still didn't hear right. She still wasn't home, so that posed a concern. A few moments later, M came banging the mail slot around, as he always did. I let him in and told him what's going on. He seemed fairly concerned and said he'd stick around. He offered to drive to where the party thing was, but I didn't even have an address.

Me and M played video games, watched movies, and laughed at bad music videos until after midnight. We ordered a pizza and made the best of a bad situation. What could I tell the cops, I think she is somewhere in the state, and she might be at a candle sale, or dead in a gutter somewhere? M did offer to take me to where she was, but it wasn't much help since I didn't know where, and she wasn't with family.

I called again after 1. This was super late, and I was even getting tired. She finally picked up the phone. "What?! What do you want!?" I apparently did something wrong. I asked her where she was. "Upper Marlboro. I'm with my friend Joseph. His cat died, and he needed a friend." To set the stage for distance, Upper Marlboro, MD, is approximately an hour and a half away from the apartment, to even hit the outskirts of town. Hell, from where I live now, which is much further south than I was, it's still almost an hour. "Why are you even down there this late? Why didn't you tell me where you were going?" She just treated me like I had done something wrong. "Because you would have been mad at me if I did."

Most of the time, if you think someone would be mad at you if you did something, it's probably a bad thing to do. At this moment, I was wrong for even asking. I again asked her to come home. "It's super late. I'll drive home in the morning. Don't worry, we didn't do anything. His mom is super nice." If you have to tell me you didn't do anything, what do you think I'll think given the circumstances? Also, I don't care if his mom is nice. She said she would see me tomorrow, she was tired, and hung up on me. Thankfully, she was on speaker, and M heard the whole thing. He opted to stay the night and just crash on the couch.

The next morning, we woke up and went out for Burger King. Ok, I know what you're thinking, and no, I wasn't sponsored by BK, or have an obsession with it. M didn't want McDonald's, and BK was the next option. We dined on breakfast food, and around 10 in the morning and M drove us back to the apartment. We pulled into a space around the corner and walked to my house. As we rounded the corner, I saw my wife's gold Saturn parked in our spot. When we approached a little closer, we noticed there was a passenger in the car. She fucking brought Joseph along for the ride. I was more pissed off he was there, but even more infuriated that she would have to take him home. He spotted us and immediately reached around the car, locking all the locks, and reclined his seat back as if to hide.

Now, to set the scene for you to get a visual of what had just approached our little friend. I was wearing some grungy shirt I found at a store in Arizona, jeans, had a high and tight. M, because I'm sure it helps with the visual, was black. He had dreads. He had a goatee and was wearing his finest hood Sean John apparel. We didn't look too friendly approaching the car, and we were fine with that. The secret is, M is a teddy bear of a guy, and the nicest dude you'll ever meet, but Joseph didn't need to know that. Marvin sat on the car hood and mean mugged him pretty hard. He told me he had this, go inside, and get my girl.

I went into the apartment, and my wife was messing with a small backpack full of stuff. I was furious. "Welcome home. Nice of you to join me." She stared at me. "You would do the same for your friends so why is it not ok for me?" Clearly, she didn't see the issue and immediately changed subjects. "We are going to go see Twilight. Do you want to join us?" I stared in disbelief that those words came out of her skull just now. "One: Never. Ever. Neverever never invite me to Twilight. I don't want to see the sparkly vampires. B: Did you just invite your husband as the third wheel on your little movie date?" She didn't have a good answer. "Look, if you're going to be a jerk to me, fine. I'll just stay down at Joseph's again!" and stormed out the door. "Oh, I see your little butt buddy is here. You'll be fine. Cuddle with him you faggot." With that, she jumped in her car and the two of them headed off to the movies.

Now, I know what you're thinking. Shouldn't I have ended it there? The answer is yes. Had I have ended everything there, we wouldn't have the next several chapters, for one. It would also show that I am not an idiot, which I clearly was. My remaining three days went by, and I flew back down and resumed my training. Graduation was shortly after Valentine's Day, so that was just around the corner.

I received my duty station, which was going to be where I lived for the next few years; Fort Bliss, TX. No idea where that was, but I had watched Walker: Texas Ranger and King of the Hill, so I knew a thing or two about Texas. Turns out, neither prepared me for what I was about to enter. I finished training, graduated, and flew back home to set up the movers to move our belongings. When I arrived home, it was a mess. Laundry everywhere, dishes all over. Mounds of trash and the cat box was a mountain of turds. We only had one cat, so how is this an issue? Since the Army messed up on plane tickets and travel, our flight was canceled, and we were driving down. The Army frowns upon tardiness, so we hit the road, packing some clothes, ourselves and the cat.

CHAPTER 10

Call Of Doody

We hit the road, driving all the way from Maryland to West Texas. All in all, the drive took three days. Her family helped coordinate a place to live also! She had a second aunt a few times removed or something, and she owned a rental home. We were bound for the house. On the ride down, my wife was pretty bitchy, but I ignored it. I figured I'd be in a bad mood if I had to drive us across the country too, but I can't drive, so here we are.

We get to Dallas, everything looks peachy. There were trees, grass, just the same as I had seen back home. Then we entered the sandy nothingness once again. Son of a bitch. I'm back in the sand? I must be cursed. We arrive in the city limits, and her aunt, our future landlord, called her phone to tell us to meet her and her husband at the house as they were waiting. We made it there, and they drove us to Chico's Tacos, a local specialty taco spot. We got to know each other, and they seemed ok. She said we could get set up in the house when we got back. Since it's late in the day, we can sign paperwork tomorrow. Sweet, off to a good start. We had our tacos, got to know each other, and returned back to the house to catch some sleep.

We signed the lease the next morning. Looking at it, the

contract appeared to be a template snagged from the internet. There were a ton of grammar errors and a lot of continuity issues with the paragraphs. It honestly looked like someone doctored up a document they downloaded. We had agreed on the rent and signed on the dotted line. Her aunt also mentioned she was not going to be removing the furniture she had in the house, it would stay. Ok, whatever, we can work around it since we didn't have much furniture with the roof collapse and small townhouse, to begin with. We received our keys and got settled. My wife drove me on base to begin my in-processing phase, so I could get to my unit and get this ball rolling.

The base itself was massive. I mean, you could wander off and never be seen again type of massive. Luckily, when you do this processing business, they cart you around by van to get you to each of the locations each day. My wife was taking me on base each day around 8, and she would pick me up around 3 or 4 once we completed everything. This process went on for about a week or so, trying to get my medical records updated, my personal files up to speed, and overall learning how to do this soldier thing now that I'm out of training. My wife bonded fairly ok with the landlord, who helped her track down the grocery stores and fun spots to go to in town, which I thought was pretty cool of her. After my processing phase, I was off to my actual unit, with the guys I'd be working with for quite a while.

I was delivered to my headquarters, which was almost a half hour away from the main base, over on an airfield. I was to be part of First Armored Division, the Dirty Dorito, as they joked to me. I didn't know anything about these inside jokes, but it was kinda funny. I was dropped off in front of this massive building and escorted to the office I needed to report to. I finalized what I needed to do for the unit, and I was in. It was time to meet the man in charge of me, my squad leader. This is the guy, or gal, who is supposed to train me up, get me up to speed, and be accountable for my actions and whereabouts. Thankfully, I'm pretty uneventful, quiet, and don't get into too much trouble, so this guy should have no issues with me. I get walked across the street, to our storage room, where I am introduced to Sergeant Ullrich. He kind of looked like a low rent version of Liev Schreiber, which was funny since the Wolverine movie came out around that time, making that actor super relevant. He gave me the lowdown on how he operates. He was very similar to my management style at my last job; show me respect, don't lie, and communicate. I can dig it.

Sgt Ullrich and I worked together for quite a while, as I was his only soldier for the squad. It's pretty easy to be the focus when there is no competition for attention. He made sure I was all set up with everything because we were headed to a field training exercise right away. This first one took me through my birthday, I turned twenty-four in the middle of the desert of El Paso, away from anyone I really knew. I wasn't really close to anyone in the unit at this time, but there were a few interesting characters that I was sure to connect with. We returned from the field, and a few weeks went by, with my wife still driving me to work daily. One morning, sometime in April, she said "I'm not waking up to take your ass. I have a busy day." She didn't work, she was planning on shopping, again, and spending my money. I ended up late to work after I battled to have her take me. Now, the Army is not the place you want to show up late for. Thankfully, Sgt. Ullrich was able to work me out of a trouble spot. He told our first sergeant, who was the head honcho, that I was going to get my damn driver's license.

Once we were off the hook for me being late, he told me to get in the car. I got into his car, and we rode out to the DMV, which was my first taste of how most of the non-deployed army life goes. I walked in and tried to take the test. The test only costs about 25 bucks, which was a huge shocker, considering how much everything was in Maryland. I signed up to start the ordeal. Everything was solid, and we were moving along just fine, however, there was one speed bump; I didn't bring my glasses for the eye exam. Now, I don't usually wear my glasses, and considering I shot perfect accuracy at the range without them, I figured I was doing pretty solid. Unfortunately for me, that was the no go for the DMV, and they said to come back when I was prepared. Considering this was an impromptu visit, no harm done.

We went back a few days later, and I passed the eye exam, and the written, apart from one question. "In a vehicle, who are required to wear seatbelts? Driver only, Front Seat, No One, or Everyone?" I answered Everyone, and I was wrong. In Maryland, it's everybody, but apparently, in Texas, people in the backseat safety be damned! I took the actual drivers test, and I failed. The lady was very abrasive, and not really pleasant. She had me open the windows up, air conditioning off, and the radio off. No distractions, I guess. She failed me, but apparently, I get three tries with that twenty bucks! I returned again a week later and gave it a shot once more. I got the same damn woman. What are the odds? She failed me again, and I was down to my last try. It was the last time my Sergeant was going to take me there.

I managed to convince my wife to let me borrow the car. I had given it a few test spins, taking myself up to the mountain canyon down the road, for our off base physical fitness days. I felt I was able to get a handle on things and knew the car a little bit and that should help me pass the test. I went to the DMV, signed in, and prepared to fail for the third time. The first time, I lost points for speeding through a school zone that wasn't even labeled. The signs had been removed, but the neighborhood must have known that was a school area. Not me, since I didn't live over there, and I was still new to El Paso. The second time, I took my turn a bit too wide, which I attributed to the fact I was driving military vehicles long before I had a license. This time, I was ready for this lady. I was told to park the car in the starting position and wait for the instructor. I grabbed the car, got in the spot, having already turned the air off, opened windows, and turned off the radio in prep. The instructor came to my vehicle and asked me to step out while they did a visual inspection. It was a different lady, and it was a refreshing change of pace. We inspected the vehicle, seat belted up and prepared for the test.

The first thing she asked is "Why is the air conditioning off, is it broken?" I told her it worked fine, and the other lady wanted it off. I assumed that was the standard. We rolled up the windows and cranked the AC, which was honestly a game changer since I wasn't sweating the whole time like previous tests. We drove forward, went in reverse, then did parallel parking. After we parked, she said, "It's pretty quiet, do you listen to music while you are in the car?" With that, I turned the radio on low. This was nice, as we hit the block, finished the test, and parked. She said there were some things to work on, but overall not bad, and I got my driver's license! This was a proud day, and you have no idea how freeing this was to me. I drove home, very excited to share the news. I also texted my sergeant to let him know the ordeal. The next thing to do was to get a vehicle.

I received a huge chunk of my Army enlistment bonus. I must have received almost 9 grand in one lump sum, which was the most money I had ever seen in my bank account at any time. I wanted to use the money to buy a car, or at least put money down on one. I also wanted a TV and a sound system, because I love my electronics. I purchased a flat screen 47-inch Sharp tv, and a surround sound system. I was on top of the world. Since I got floor models, I barely paid a grand for both. Now, remember, this was 2009, TVs of this size were considered huge and very expensive, so I came out ahead, given the time. My wife, she blew my money on a purebred Pug. It cost 5 grand for this damn dog because she had a pedigree certification and was a breeding dog or something. She then paid 300 bucks or so to have it fixed. This dog was stupid, and a stupid waste of money. At least I still had some funds to buy a car, right?

I then checked my account and noticed there was another purchase. She purchased a bird. A Conure, to be exact. A damn parrot. She had to get a cage as well, to include all of its accessories like it was a damn Barbie doll. Turns out, the cage was 700 bucks, the food and other toys were another 300, and the damn bird was almost 2 grand itself. My money flitted away so fast, and long story short, the bird died pretty quick. I'll spare you the update that you'll probably read about a paragraph or two later in the story, and just say she didn't feed it, neglected it, and it died. I don't know birds, nor do I know what they need. I had about 500 bucks or so left to put down on a car.

I went to a dealership that weekend and picked up a Chevrolet Cavalier for super cheap. It was red and black, my two favorite colors. The best part was that it only cost me 4 grand, for a car with barely 30 thousand miles on it. I loved this car. I may have loved the car more than my wife. It had a cd player, a radio, and all the things a car should have. My wife hated that car, as she begrudgingly took photos of me with the car, as I made my worst supermodel poses over it. So now at this point, we had our own vehicles, she was free to go where she needed to go, sleep in when needed, and all of that good stuff. We were moving on up.

Shortly after obtaining my vehicle, I got severely injured. While running one morning with our commander, she went off the road in the dirt, we were running on both concrete and dirt at the same time, really uneven and unstable stuff. Now I was a stupid fast runner, a damn gazelle. I could run the two-mile run in less than nine minutes. I was fast. Which was my problem, because as I was hauling around, I rolled off the concrete, into the dirt. What would have been a rolled ankle, turned into practically rolling my whole hip and leg, and landing hard on the ground. I wanted to die. A few people turned to check on me and noticed I couldn't get up. I was helped up, and long story short, I really messed up my hip, which is still a battle I fight with the VA today. One of the off-post hospitals told me I had a fracture, and I was not deployable. Well, now I feel like a waste.

Injury aside, I had to make up for my shortcomings with academic performance. I tried to do all I could on paper to compensate for what I lacked physically, with my lack of running. The worst part is that being non-deployable, it was all for nothing. I'm not going to do my job, nor am I ever going to use this useless knowledge I'm stocking up on. My wife seemed indifferent on my deployment status, which she should have been happy to hear I wasn't going to combat. I pushed through my injury and tried to stay on top of my physical therapy and everything. I still wanted to go to Iraq or something. It's part of the experience, I felt.

In May, we had a major issue. It was a weekend, and I was home cleaning a virus from my computer due to downloading music or something from one of those programs like LimeWire, as you did back in the day. When I'm in a virus removal mode, I am in the zone, unaware of what is going on in my world. I started to smell some smoke. I paused what I was doing and went off to investigate what was the matter. I headed from the spare bedroom over to the kitchen. The stove was ablaze. There was a pan with food in it, that was now charcoal, with fire on top. My wife was nowhere to be found. I immediately handled the fire situation, burning at least three dishrags and my arm hair in the process, but it was contained. My adrenaline was pumping, my heart racing. Where the hell was my woman?

I started screaming her name, and she didn't answer. I looked around the whole house, out the back door, and finally out the front door. I see her, standing on the corner, on her cell phone. I screamed to her to get the hell back to the goddamn house. I understand I was yelling, I just battled a damn house fire. She made her way back to the house, and I was livid. I started demanding to know who she was talking to that was so important that she forgot she was making food. I also wanted to know why it was so secretive that she couldn't have the conversation inside the house. "Who the hell were you talking to?" I asked. She told me it was her friend, Tim. Ok, I guess it was a guy from a job she worked at because she sure as hell doesn't really know anyone down here. She said it's cool, he lives in Florida or something now. I was still pissed. We were shouting and yelling, which was at least eighty percent from me. The cops arrived a few moments later. In the span of the next thirty minutes after the fire, my wife called the cops, grabbed a restraining order, and had me removed from my home. My mind was racing.

I called Sergeant Ullrich to let him know what was going down. We immediately went off to the barracks housing to see about temporary arrangements. They managed to get me into a temporary room, with one of the guys in our unit that usually kept to himself. I didn't want to deal with people much after that. I shut myself in and didn't go anywhere on the weekend. I didn't leave the bed. Coincidentally, it was a holiday four-day weekend, so there was even more time off. I went nowhere. This was the first time that there was any inkling of a major issue. I don't like being penalized for things I didn't do, and this was yet another time this happened. One of the guys I befriended in the unit, Erik, hung out with me as much as he could. we played Rock Band and Guitar Hero, and even Sergeant Ullrich joined us a few times. They tried to make the best of it. We went out to play paintball and other things to get me out of my decision to hermitize in that room.

A few days went by, and I still needed some of my belongings, to make my barracks stay a bit better. Sergeant Ullrich had tried to step in as often as possible and worked his hardest to get me back into the house but to no avail. He really did go above and beyond to try to help his soldiers, and I stand by that statement, even after he got a second soldier. We were given permission by the higher-ups to escort me there and get some necessities. We headed down, and we were in the house for no more than a few minutes, when the landlord called my phone. She was insulting me, screaming obscenities and belittling me. She went off, saying I shouldn't be anywhere near that house and I have no right. She then unleashed a tirade of insults and threats.

Sergeant Ullrich couldn't take it. He grabbed my phone and introduced himself. She demanded to know what his relevance was to this. He said he was in my chain of command and it was his responsibility to ensure the welfare of his soldiers. She then started to just scream and insult him. It must have skyrocket his blood pressure, because he was hung up on and screamed out "fucking bitch!" and tossed my phone across the room. It was my phone. But I get how he was feeling; this woman just showed her crazy.

We returned back to work, with a few of my things in tow, which helped me a bit. After dropping them off in my room, we were told to report to our first sergeant's office right away. We went over and were immediately blindsided by the craziest thing to come out of the left field. She had us in the office together for a bit, and individually as well, in order to sort out the issue. Apparently, my landlord, my wife's aunt, called our unit and reported that Sergeant Ullrich was posing as our commander. We did our best to explain he said the words "in his chain of command," but she wasn't hearing it. He was clearly posing as a military officer, according to the report. He was facing a lot of trouble, and this was the first time my problems spilled over to become someone else's problems. Thankfully, at the end of the day, no action was taken on the poor guy who was just doing his job.

One day, I got a text from my wife. She said she was at the barracks and was coming to pick me up to take me home. I immediately called Sergeant Ullrich and told him what was up. He advised against it, but it's my life, so I could do what I want. He thought it would be a bad idea. He came out of a rough divorce a few months before I came to the unit. He was still pretty freshly scorned and didn't want to see the same thing happen to me. I told him that the whole cops thing was a misunderstanding, and it went out of hand. I moved back to the house.

At some point, I needed a colonoscopy. Yes, I was being roto rootered. The procedure was simple, but the prep was absolute torture. I shat so much that my body was trying to find things to expel. On one occasion, I passed out. My wife didn't so much as offer concern. For wanting me back so bad, it really didn't seem that way. After my operation of having my plumbing snaked, she took me home. I hadn't eaten in a day or so and was super hungry. I was also doped up on happy meds that they used to put me under still. Burger King, yes, again, was the meal of choice. We got my meal and headed home. I opened the car door and staggered out onto the sidewalk.

I had zero control of my motor functions. It was like being near blackout drunk. You know the phase; where you say things you don't mean, and basically take a back seat while your body goes on autopilot. I had left my burgers in the car. She tossed the bag of food, and my drink at me from the car, and sped off to see her little friend. There I was, laying in my yard, food scattered all over, and had to ride out almost two hours until I regained enough motor function to get in the house and pass out on the couch.

The next little bit of time was fairly uneventful. She started going to a church down in the city sometime in August, around the time I went to California for deployment readiness training. I wasn't deploying, but I still had to tag along for the month. While out there, I manned a dump truck with an army buddy. During my free time, I tried to call and chat with my wife as often as possible. There were a few instances where she told me she was busy, and others that she didn't answer. I survived the month of training and headed back home around mid-September. It was nice to be back home. My wife had made a friend, some girl, Agustina, I think. Something to that effect. It was nice to hear that she made a friend because that gave her something to do. They were shopping buddies, and I really hoped this wasn't Feline Junior.

A change in command staff brought us two dudes as our commander and first sergeant. One was an ex-pro wrestler, and the other was a good ol' boy from Arkansas. We also got a new guy in the unit. He oversaw the other half of our section. When they told me his name, I couldn't believe it. We were getting Sergeant Slaughter added to our team. I half expected the GI Joe or wrestler to waltz in the door, but instead, it was some stocky black dude. Slaughter was different from Ullrich in that he was extremely chill and laid back, whereas Ullrich was energetic and peppy. It was a solid balance to the team.

My platoon sergeant approached me one day and said I was deployable. She spoke to a few people, made a few calls, got things switched up, and said to be ready to go to Iraq in a few weeks. I didn't get to enjoy Halloween since I was packing. I was going to Iraq. It's a complete shock to the system to go from not going to combat, to suddenly coming to terms with it in the span of two weeks. My wife seemed pretty happy, but she said she needed something to do. She wanted to use my GI-Bill, for education to become a registered nurse. It's a massive ordeal to transfer that thing to a new person, and I didn't have the time. I wasn't going to use it, because school is dumb, or so I believed at the time. She had already been fired from a caretaker job she held for a week because she threw the old lady to the ground, or she fell, or something. Either way, the old lady was banged up pretty good, and she shouldn't be allowed to watch after a rock. I said once I get settled, I'll talk to the education office to see what I need to do for transferring my benefits to her.

The final two weeks consisted of me really doing much of nothing Since we were deploying, we would show up for work and be dismissed super early to allow time with family and all that. About a week in, I get a knock on the door. I answered it, and it was El Paso's finest waiting there. I asked if I could help them. "Mr. Carpenter?" Yeah, that's me. "We received a distress call that someone fitting your description was stalking our complainant." She called the police on me for being home from work too much. Again, you're probably thinking "Ding ding ding! Red flag, idiot!" but I didn't hear that. I had a few days in the country and didn't feel like dealing with this. The cops advised me to keep vigilant and left after realizing I lived in the house and had every right to be there. Now, it was time to get away from this crazy girl, off to Iraq!

CHAPTER 11

The Sandbox

We pick up the tale the day I shipped off. My wife drove me to work one last time. There were so many family members and friends out there, it was crazy. The reality is that this could be the last time you would see some of us. For a few of us, unfortunately, it was. So, in a sentimental fashion, I unloaded my carry-on items, and she drove off. She left me almost immediately, no real goodbye, nothing. I know it was like 4 am, but damn. She sped off like she had someone after her.

We hung around until almost 10 AM. Families stuck around and chatted. I got to meet some moms and dads, wives, and husbands. I tried not to remain bitter, but I was honestly a little pissed off. We took our belongings and made our way to the plane and prepared to debark on an adventure to the Middle East. After what felt like the world's longest plane ride, we arrived in the country of Kuwait. It was a whole lot of nothing, full of sand and hot. Honestly, it felt like we didn't go anywhere and circled Texas for a day. We were given our orders and were dismissed for the day. Everyone was exhausted Most of everyone passed out asleep.

For the next few days, we did some Army things. It was the

worst heat you could imagine, and it rained. It rained nonstop forming giant lakes around the living quarters. After completing the gun range training, we were cut loose for the day. I went to the USO tent and used a computer to check out the world and all of the goings on. I checked the bank account to see what the damage was after payday. There was a charge for 240 bucks to Olive Garden. What the hell did she get there that cost that much? Better have been a damn good wine. I had to wait until later to call. The time difference thing was still new to me.

I finally had the chance to call, and I went right for the issue. "Oh, I took everyone to Olive Garden. My grandparents, Noni, my Aunt, My Cousin, Feline..." She kept naming names. I am literally going to combat so we can show off by blowing my money on everyone. She drove off to Maryland as soon as I was wheels up, apparently. I let it go because after all, I wasn't going to be spending much money out here myself. I tried to call regularly while in Kuwait, always checking in to make sure she was ok. She was going to be staying with family in Maryland, I guess, while our house and all of our belongings sat abandoned in Texas.

I eventually made my way to Iraq. I got settled in, and the first half of the deployment goes by quite well, that is, until around March. I was in constant communication with my wife. We used Skype and Facebook to keep in touch fairly often. I had received a notification in my email that my car payment increased by several hundred dollars. As it turns out, the bank needs to have insurance, otherwise, they apply their own. I had insurance. I immediately called and found out they terminated my coverage since I deployed. That stupid gecko is supposed to be all about the military, right?

I called the bank, and they said I had to come in person to fix it. I begged and pleaded with my wife to go back to Texas and sort this out before they repossessed my car. She said she didn't feel like it. Luckily, in all of my efforts, I asked them to not action anything until I got there. Having no insurance wasn't going to hurt me. It's not like I was driving around right now. My wife was, and I had to get it sorted out quick. I finally was able to video conference with one of the representatives at the bank, and they sorted their end out. I spoke with a person at the insurance company who actually gave a damn and reinstated my insurance, considering it was still being paid.

My mid-tour leave was supposed to be in May. I liked it that way, smack in the middle of the deployment. I really didn't have a bad time out there, all things considered. If you take away the incoming rockets, gunfire, explosions, and chaos, it's quite charming. I was flying back to Texas because I wanted to bring some junk home and bring other stuff back with me. My wife was less than thrilled with that decision. She had started to act differently toward me. It may have been the separation, or maybe I was just able to see things differently.

It was time to head home. I packed my luggage and boarded the first plane out of that armpit. It took forever since I was held up trying to leave the country for almost a week. I finally had my flight and scooted off back to the States. Thankfully, they don't count your vacation time until you arrive in the country. My layover was in Dallas, and that's where they started the clock. My wife had driven down and not been happy about it. She begrudgingly picked me up from the airport and sped off from the terminal. "It's nice to see you, too." She barely said two words. She dumped me off at the house and said she was hanging out with Agustina. I was alone, yet again.

I didn't know anyone that wasn't already overseas. I knew neighbors, vaguely. There were a few soldiers left behind that were non-deployable, but not many I interacted with. The first thing I did was jump in my car, ready to hit the town. I jammed the key in, and the car didn't start. The battery was dead. She didn't start it like I asked her to because she fled off to Maryland for a while. I managed to hail a cab, get the new battery, and change it out. I didn't live far from the auto part store, thankfully. Up and running again, I hit the town.

The next day, we decided to go to the mall. I ran into two of the girls in my unit that were on the rear detachment, manning the fort while we were deployed. My wife just acted snooty with them as she always did with anyone I knew. When we got home from the mall, she jumped in her car and headed to her friend's house. She was either between seeing her friend, or our landlord. Considering I was back from Iraq, you think she'd be spending time with me, not the people you can see any day of the week. That night she told me she was staying the night to do girl things, which I wasn't worried about. I went outside to wash my car. I felt it was therapeutic and still do.

As I was setting up to wash my Chevy, the elderly neighbor from across the street noticed me. He had to be like a hundred years old and he fought in WW2. I always find it fascinating to talk to people from a different era of war and see so many similarities in what we do when we are bored. Swapping stories is always a great pastime, and I figured I was due for one.

After he took six years to leave his yard, I noticed he was headed my way. I stopped what I was doing and went to him. We talked for a bit. I told him I had deployed and was back for a few days until I am forced to go back into it. He said, "It's really good your brother came to visit and keep her company a few weeks ago." Wait, what? "A stocky blond feller, with spiky hair. It was a bit strange. They were holding hands a lot." Well, her brother had long black hair, and my brother is too poor and useless to fly out here. Who is blondie? I had another neighbor who told me the same a few days later. Seemed like something I should investigate further, right?

I asked her about it when she did come back to the house

two days later. She told me not to worry about it. Most of my vacation was spent alone. I flew back out and made it back to Iraq safely. I called my wife shortly after I began my first shift to check on things. Usually, when I called, it was around 4 pm her time, so I knew it was a decent time to call. She picked up the phone "What the hell do you want? I'm driving!" I asked where she was going. "I'm going back to Maryland, and thanks to you I missed my exit and I'm halfway through Georgia." For one, no path back home takes you anywhere near Georgia. It was my fault she didn't know north from south.

CHAPTER 12

War. War Never Changes,
But People Do

I had only been in the country a short few weeks, and already I had annoyed her and pissed her off, according to my wife. My constant calling every day, my annoying emails, and Facebook messages were driving her up the wall. I assumed that communication was the thing to do, but I started cutting back and even stopped calling nightly. While all of this was going on, everyone else seemed to communicate with their spouse on a regular basis. I spoke to my friends more than I did her. It was an odd predicament to be stuck in.

As time went on, it must have been sometime mid-June at this point, I was working at my vehicle which was located a few minutes away from our office. The story on paper was, I was performing recon and surveillance on the truck and area. I was out patrolling the perimeter when from the sky came a rocket that landed a sneeze away from me. In truth, I was taking a leak on the concrete barricade outside of my truck's area, and the rocket came down. Had I not been going pee, I would have done it in my pants. I could have died.

I went back to the office to report to Sergeant Ullrich right away. I told him there was incoming fire on the base. A moment later the intercom blared "INCOMING! INCOMING!" over the loudspeakers. I jokingly said "Yeah. No shit. What that guy said" and stated what happened. We had to jazz up the story a bit, because, taking a whizz on the barricade was frowned upon. After we were allowed back on the phones and the internet, I called my wife to tell her how I almost died. I figured it's something you share with your spouse.

She didn't care. She seemed very indifferent and not concerned at all. I didn't even get an "Oh my god! Are you ok?" out of her or anything. She was just fairly meh on the whole subject. She also gave a similar reaction when bullets rained down on us too. I had started to notice a trend, and it wasn't a very good one. Don't think this was the peak of the second half of my deployment at all. It got much worse from here.

These were the days of the transition from Myspace to Facebook for social media. Good times those were, and I maintained both pages pretty well. I happened to get a message on Myspace from some girl. I had no idea who the heck it was, but she messaged me a hell of a paragraph or two. I have the original message, but I'll paraphrase to the best of my ability.

"Hello, I hope this is the right Harry Carpenter in the Army because I know your wife. She has been sleeping with my husband, and I have proof. I really hope you are the right guy. Please reach out to me. She is tearing up my marriage and ruined my family. I have a son."

I sat back wondering what the hell was going on, so I called my wife. I asked her what was up with this girl and what is going on. She responded "Oh, that girl is crazy. I got a restraining order on her. I don't know what her deal is." I said I was going to get involved if her safety was a concern. I needed to take measures on my end as well. I can let the military police know, the local police also. She said "This isn't your problem Stay out of it. I'll take care of it." She was very dismissive of the whole thing. She hung up with me, but I wasn't satisfied. Sergeant Ullrich decided it was time to Sherlock this thing out on the internet.

We devoted several hours to look into this girl, her profile, and any detail we could find out. We got her profile info. It said she lived in Florida. Wow, I think that is a hell of a trip to Texas or Maryland to be a psycho stalker. Her marital status was confirmed as married and has a few photos with her kid. Everything checked out. Myspace never had a "married to" with a direct link to their profile like Facebook but chances were her husband was in the top eight. We did a bit of digging. We looked through the whole profile and finally, there he was: tagged in a photo. Ullrich found him.

There, buried among a ton of photos of the Florida setting, among beaches and girl squad pictures, it was found. A family photo. Clearly labeled with names, taken from the past Christmas. Ullrich dug deeper and rooted out a name from the profile. He also found his profile as well. Tim. We dubbed him Tim the Enchanter, which I have been unable to forget to this day. Tim. I knew this name. Why did I know this name? He turned his laptop around to show me what this Tim the Enchanter looked like. All of it came fluttering back at me like a vacuum had been reversed in my soul. He was a stocky build. Blonde, spiky hair. His name was Tim. This was the guy from the phone call last year. This was the guy at my house in May. This was the guy she was sleeping around with. I tried my hardest to dismiss it since the pieces were too easy to put together. I needed to hear it from her, and that wasn't happening.

A few days later, my mom and I talked on the phone. She said my brother got a message on Myspace from a girl who claimed my wife was banging her man. I never responded to the girl, so I guess she moved on to family accounts. The letter more or less detailed the same thing. My mom still has a printed copy in her house somewhere, among a few other crazy things

I'm sure. That's two people she reached out to. Given the name, physical description, it's hard to deny what was going on.

My mom had the best interactions with my wife while I was deployed. I didn't talk to her often, so I was shotgun blasted with the information during phone calls. She didn't stay up late and worked all day, so it was hard to time those calls. She filled me in on all the adventures and crazy excitement I was missing out on. Back in the winter, my wife was up in Maryland. She was helping my mom out by driving her to work. My mom gave her gas money and everything for her time, but it was a drive from her family to mine each day. She would stay at my mom's occasionally.

One day, she was staying over my mom's house. She had just gotten there when her dad called and said she needed to come to his house and make dinner. She apparently had a nervous break. She started screaming in tongues, breaking some of my mom's things in a rage fit. She stormed out of the house. She ended up hitting a snowbank with the car on the way to her dad's. This was news to me.

She also told me about the time my wife was driving my mom to the mall, and they were pulled over. My wife had a suspended license apparently. The officer was friendly and cooperative, but my wife was an idiot. "You can't give me a ticket, I'm Army!" The officer asked where she was stationed, her unit, and everything. She blanked, and said, "Oh, my husband is military." He wasn't happy with that either because she was stalling. The officer asked if my mom had a license to drive the car home, and my wife refused to cooperate with this guy. She wouldn't let my mom touch the wheel of the car. The ultimatum was given; my mom drives or the car is towed. In hindsight, the car should have been towed and my mom called a cab. At the time, my mom fought with her to let her drive. My wife had a suspended license for speeding through a school zone, failure to stop at a stop sign, cutting off a school bus, and not appearing in court for the hearing. Fun times.

In addition to the car business, she went into a diabetic coma or something. My mom stayed with her in the hospital, and she was in there for almost a week. I didn't know any of this. Turns out her blood sugar was near a thousand, which I'm told is really bad. They stabilized her, and she eventually came to. They set her up with a nutritionist to discuss her diet. She said she knew what she is doing. She was going to continue to eat all of the cheese curls, potato chips, and candy she wanted. She said that the doctor was an idiot. She proceeded to insult the doctors because as you know, she was the expert on all things diabetes after coming out of a diabetic coma.

So, I learned an earful of information about her little trips to Maryland. She had a guy during her ocean visit and suspended licenses. It clicked also, the day she went to Georgia by accident, she was actually headed to or from Florida to see Tim the Enchanter. It's not like I could track her location, but she felt the need for an alibi. Maybe she thought I could phone in a favor and dedicate a satellite to spy on her, who knows. The pieces were starting to come together. Sergeant Ullrich insisted I begin a divorce process. I hadn't quite gotten to that point mentally or emotionally, but I was close. I didn't want to believe it was going on. My rational side began preparing my brain for what was to come.

Sometime around her birthday, near the end of July, she posted up the typical "Birthday Adventures" post. You know the type. "Woke up. Ate at my favorite place. Did this, that, and the other. Great birthday. Thanks, everyone." She wrote her plans out, and I happened to comment on it, poking fun at a typo. I still do this to people, especially if it cracks me up. Her friend Feline commented and said I was disrespectful. I was immediately attacked by her, my wife, and several hero guy friends to the rescue. All I did was disrespected by cracking a joke that did not insult or attack her character or person. I saw nothing wrong.

This message thread boiled over into having my friends and hers posting comments. It led to Feline and a few others to disrespect the military. That there is a big no-no. Feline said she hopes I get blown up in Iraq because she is sick of me and hopes these loser friends do too. I even got death threats from my wife's dad on my Facebook. Thankfully he couldn't spell and said, "I can't wait until you come home from Iraq so I can test your comat skills!" What's a comat? At any rate, the insults toward the military and threats toward me set off a few of my sergeants who were mutual friends or could at least see the post. It got ugly, and ultimately, I was blocked on Facebook by my wife. I still am blocked to this day.

She still took phone calls and said she blocked me because she didn't like how that thread turned out. I told her that it was her friends that turned it ugly. She got offended that I would insult her friends. I still clung to this relationship and made it work for some reason. I was told I was going to train in another country for a week or two and geared up to fly to Qatar with three guys from my section.

We flew into the new place, and let me tell you, it was humid. We arrived late at night. It must have been 10ish. I was joined by my buddy Jim, Chris, and one of my drinking crew from training in Arizona, Rob. All in all, it was a solid crew and I couldn't think of anyone else to be saddled up with. We finally got ahold of someone at this training unit, and they misplaced the fact we were coming. The captain in charge had to scramble to set us up with something and fast. We got rooms, fed, and were on the right track. This base also had a Fox Sky bar, which served alcohol, three drink maximum. By the time we were settled in, we found out it was closing in 15 minutes and Jim and I sprinted to the building and slammed three drinks. This was an amazing time.

Turns out, we were forgotten about. The Air Force unit training us had to book a flight physical, among other things, and we got to hang around for a total of four weeks. That was four weeks of Air Force accommodations like alcohol, a pool, and a shopping mall, among the various Air Force luxuries. We used the 24-hour gym and dining facilities. This was absolute paradise. Apparently, we could have rented jet skis, done boat tours, and so much more, but we didn't. Me and Jim bonded well and became gym buddies. I went from 135 lbs. up to a beautiful 170 lbs. of muscle by the time we left this place. Life was good.

My anniversary came up in the middle of the trip, so I looked online for a gift to ship. This was before Amazon was really a thing. I found a nice jewelry box or something. I had it customized our names and anniversary information and shipped it off. I didn't tell her because she barely talked to me. I thought it was a pretty killer gift, considering my resources available to me. A week or so went by and I heard nothing. No phone call, nothing. She was headed back to Texas, so I assumed she was driving a lot. I timed the package to be there around the time she arrived. She eventually sent me a message to my Skype to tell me she made it safe. We rounded out our training, more like a second vacation, and flew back to our base.

I arrived back being the only one without sunburn from drinking and passing out in the pool. I was too busy trying to contact my significant other to float around a pool after a few beers. The real show started the last two months, and it was brutal. While I was out, Sergeant Ullrich discovered on my wife's Facebook page an album of underwear shoots. She did a bunch of these shoots, it seemed, and they were dated back to before we even moved. They were hidden to me, so I never even knew of them. He showed me what he saw. During the next call, I asked her about it. She denied everything and said I am making it up, so I went ahead and described the photos in detail. She was found out, far as I was concerned.

While rooting through her news feed and other things, there was some Spanish dude, Latin Lover, who commented to a lot of her posts. He would share things like "I had fun" and stuff to that effect. I more or less at that point had my mind made up as to what next steps to take. Divorce while overseas was not in the cards. I wanted to be home and take care of things in person, but I had to wait. The last month of my deployment was mental hell, as she blocked me on all forms of communication I had. I found out from a mutual friend she was in a nasty car accident. I couldn't do anything about it. I assumed she was ok, or they would have gone deeper into it.

By the time I flew home, I was already in a different mindset but did my best to put on a face. I flew home with a few friends since we didn't all go at once. My buddy Drew was on my flight, and he knew what was going on with me. He offered his sympathies and said if he and his wife could do anything, they would. We arrived in Georgia, where I called Sprint and activated my phone again. It felt great to be able to communicate again and to be back in the United States, even if it was just an airport terminal.

My first call was to my mom and then dad to tell them I arrived fine. Then I called my grandparents and two or three friends. You could easily see where my priorities were at. I finally called my spouse. I told her we should be in Texas by four, and there will be a ton of us coming in. She said she would try to make it, but she was with Agustina at the moment. Glad I am an afterthought, considering I was coming home from a combat zone. Some of us, again, did not come home. Be it from combat, incoming fire, or suicide.

We landed on Fort Bliss around 3 or so. They had to debrief

us and tell us all the things we needed to hear before we went off with our families. We were given the next few days off to rest, recover and decompress before unloading all of our equipment. This was going to be epic. I called my wife to tell her to find us. I texted the address and even Drew's wife offered to pick her up. She declined. After she made her way to the base and circled the area for 20 minutes, she texted me and she was furious that I was wasting her time. We sent Mallory, Drew's wife to escort her back. They finally made it to the hangar. I stashed my phone in a pocket.

We were all in formation. We didn't have our bags on us. They were stashed elsewhere and being unloaded. We marched into the neighboring hangar and were greeted by epic music like Final Countdown and Eye of the Tiger. There was fog, lasers, confetti, and balloons. What a greeting! We marched in and stood anxiously in formation. They announced over the speaker: "Families, this is an order. Hug your soldier! Soldiers, your bags are out front. Fallout! Dismissed!" Everyone went running to each other. It was a madhouse! Hugs and kisses flooded the room. Crying, laughter, and smiles were filling the room from everyone. Everyone, that is, except my wife.

She stood, arms crossed, frowning. Everyone saw her. I attempted to introduce her to some buddies and she didn't care. "Let's go. I don't have all fucking day. I have shit to do, and I can't do it wasting my day here." I asked if she wanted to go to a big dinner at a restaurant with everyone. She told me to get in the car. I went out with her to get my bags, and she almost left me because I hadn't gotten them all. Finally, they unloaded my last bag. I loaded everything up in the trunk, got in the car, and she sped off. We went straight home. No small talk, nothing. I was dropped off in front of the house, got my bags out of the car, and she drove off. What a post-deployment welcome I had.

One thing I noticed, which I didn't pay attention to because of so much commotion, was she had a new car. She no longer had the Saturn we got at CarMax a few years ago, after her Mazda was hit just before the wedding. She had a Hyundai Sonata. A whole new car. I heard about the accident while up in Maryland. The details where she was rear-ended and pushed into another car, but the damage wasn't that bad. This was a brand new, current year car. With Texas plates. She got the car here and recently. Why wasn't I ever told?

Just like that, I made it to my first day back from deployment. I was alone, holding my bags, standing in front of my house. Everyone else was with family, friends, and having a blast. I was alone, and miserable once again. We were told not to drive ourselves until we acclimated to home life again, but I don't listen very well. I loaded my bags inside, showered, and started my car. This time it started, as opposed to my mid-tour leave, and I drove off to explore the town, clear my head, and collect my thoughts.

CHAPTER 13

Baby Don't Hurt Me

What was I to do? I was alone, driving around to see all of the places I could and do my best retail therapy. I went around to all my usual haunts; Best Buy, Circuit City, Walmart, and the mall. After my little foray into retail therapy, I went home and bedded down for the night. This meant watching tv and catching up on MythBusters. I couldn't possibly find it in me to go to sleep, even though I deserved the world's longest nap. Marathoning Adam and Jamie was probably the more therapeutic thing I did after coming home from combat. I must have powered through three for four episodes when my wife finally came home. She was crying. What the hell happened? She sat down on the couch, the closest she had willingly been to me. It must have been three or four in the morning, or damn near, by the time she came home. I asked what was wrong. "I was at a party with my friend, Agustina, remember her? Well, I was there, and we were all drinking and having fun, and I fell and hit my head really hard. They put me in the bed to make sure I didn't hurt myself, and her big brother kept kissing me, and raped me." Jesus, this is the story of my life. How does she keep getting taken advantage of? I was about to go on a rampage. At the end of the day, she is still my wife. Even if she is acting like an asshole and possibly banging Tim the Enchanter.

Her friend's older brother was Mexican, just like her. I found that the family was from Mexico. Was she across the border? Where the hell did this dude live? It was November. I was trying to wind down from deployment and prepare for actually enjoying the holidays home this year. I told her I would handle this guy, but of course, she said don't worry about it. She wasn't going to be going over there again. It was quiet that night, and several nights to follow. She didn't run off out of the house the next two days on me, so we actually got to spend time together. The rest of the unit finally made it in over the course of the next week. We resumed work once again, and I started reporting for duty. We were pretty relaxed after the deployment, with unpacking and cleaning everything. We didn't have a whole lot to do, and everyone was in the mindset of block leave in December. We were going to have an entire month off. Some post-deployment vacation to spend with our families for the holidays. I never had that at any type of job before. We made it through Thanksgiving, inviting a single soldier over to spend with us. This was one of the many services I offered. Nobody should be sitting alone on a holiday. We had gone out the following day, and I updated my phone. We even managed to switch her to Sprint, keeping her number and all. Now we were on one account, grabbing discounts. I treated myself to a new Xbox 360, since my last one was not working from Iraq, a much-needed replacement. Block leave began on the 5th of December, and that's when things took a sharper turn for the worst.

I had been on leave for maybe three or four days at this point when my wife came into the room screaming at me. "Why the hell are you always home? You're pissing me off! Please go do something! Take yourself to work! I hate you being home." Wow, that was out of the left field. I told her she could just scoot out the door on her own and entertain herself if she was tired of looking at me. She did just that and picked up and hit the road. I was home alone, once again. This was when I received a call from our landlord, her aunt. "I want you out. You need to go you piece of shit." Well, how do you do? Happy day to you as well. I had no idea where this was coming from, but apparently, she filled me in. "You two have not paid rent in months. The dog needs to be removed. I do not like you." Well, that's just rude. The dog didn't do anything to anyone.

The following week, I received an eviction notice to be removed. I started searching for my rental receipts and found all of them, thankfully. A few days later, she mailed a second eviction notice, which now only included just my name. It was frustrating. My wife was upset by the first notice, but once the second one came in she seemed pretty calm about the whole thing. Something was clearly up. Everyone was on block leave and at every end of the country visiting family and friends. I didn't have any money to do anything if I wanted to since my bank account was drained. Deployment perks included combat pay, hazard duty pay, and tax-free money. I didn't have a dime of any of it anymore. I was at my wits end with how things were playing out.

My wife took off quite frequently. One of the days she was home I decided to wrangle her down, and the two of us were going to this damn landlord and sort matters out. We got in my car and drove to the other side of town, around the mountain to her home. We were also paying the rent for December, and I was going to pay it in person, so I could see it all go down. We pulled up to their condo and parked outside. The aunt and her husband came out and said she was not accepting my money because we have to go. I told her it doesn't work that way, and she better take my damn money! I was still sitting in my car, windows rolled down. She reached into my car and started choking me and calling me a faggot and asshole and saying that she should just choke the life out of me. I put the car in reverse, she let her hands go and I got out of dodge. My heart was racing, I didn't know what just happened. I was speeding away from their place, but the two of them followed close. This crazy lady even tried to run me off the road at one point. I took the car to 88 mph and sped off down the exit ramp. I must have started blacking out due to the stress and excitement because I came to and my wife was screaming and grabbing for the wheel. We were two seconds from slamming into the barricade. I immediately pulled off the next exit to the mall.

Once I stopped the vehicle my wife got out of the car, screaming for help. At first, I thought she was going to get help from this psychopath that was chasing us down in her vehicle, who just throttled me in my own car. I got out of my car to catch my breath and wind down from the whole ordeal. She screamed "help" through the parking lot and said, "My husband is trying to kill me!" I couldn't believe it. Two guys came over to save the day. They asked me what my problem was, and I told them nothing happened. But then something did. I got punched in the face. After about a 30 second beatdown by two guys in the parking lot, they pinned me down in front of my car until the cops came. With the good Samaritans present, and the cops also in attendance, her aunt rolled in like the white knight. I went to jail and was transferred to the Military Police to deal with me. Thankfully, no charges really stuck because my wife never followed up with anything. This also started a trend of calling the MPs and local police on me every ten seconds of my existence, which would go on for another 5 years.

After that ordeal blew over, my wife didn't come home for almost a week. It was two weeks before Christmas, and I was not having any fun. Supposedly, she was staying with our landlord. One day, she came home. It was later in the evening, and I know because I rented the DVD of the movie Cats and Dogs and was prepared to watch it. When she came through the house, something didn't feel right. I invited her to watch the movie with me, and I didn't hear so much as an insult. I went to investigate, you know like they do in horror movies. She was packing a bag and looked intoxicated. Did she drive here? I tried to stop her so we could talk about it.

It was at that moment I realized I made a bad choice. In the past, she had gotten physical. She had hit me fairly frequently. I'm a guy, so I just had to man up and take it because it's weak to admit that. She started throwing things at me and screaming bloody murder. I assume this was like what my mom saw during one of her breakdowns. She stormed off and grabbed a knife from the kitchen.

After wrestling the knife away, she ran off again. Keep in mind, our windows and screen door are open. It was December, but it was still 80 degrees in El Paso. The whole neighborhood could hear the screaming and shouting. Hell, all of Texas could hear us. She came up from behind and struck me with something really hard on my head, and I fell forward into the screen door. I recovered and followed after her. She went back to her car and started it. I tried to continue to talk sense into her to stop. She threw the car in drive and struck me with the car. Every single neighbor saw. She sped off, haphazardly into the distance.

The cops arrived about twenty minutes or so later. They took statements from all of the neighbors and me. They photographed my bloody scalp, my cut hands, and the bent screen door from her egress. I opted to not press charges since I still was trying to salvage something. They put a warrant out for her arrest and considered her hostile and a danger to herself and others. The neighbors put up their statements to push the charges in this direction.

It must have been an hour or so since the cops left the house. I actually blocked the front door with furniture, barricading myself inside in a way. Look, I just went to combat for a year, and I was fairly terrified. I had no idea what she was thinking or what her next move was. There was activity at the door. She unlocked it and gave a serious shove. She came in and sat down on the couch and apologized for her behavior. She seemed off still. A few moments later, there was a knock on the door. Two officers came in, arresting her right away.

She looked directly at me. "You called the fucking police, you pussy?" The cops told her to calm down and be quiet. "I didn't do anything wrong! I wouldn't hurt anyone!" The officers again told her to calm down, cuffed her and stood her up to walk out. She asked if she could have her purse, and they agreed. I mentioned she is diabetic, and I was going to put the insulin in her purse and get it for her. She looked at me again, this time with malice. "You smug little fucker. I'll slit your throat when I get back tonight." Wow, those are not the things to yell in front of cops. They dragged her out and took her to the station. I felt more uneasy than ever before.

I went to bed on the couch that night. I slept with the TV on and honestly, I wouldn't even call it sleep. The next morning, I felt like I had to do something. I got dressed and headed out to the police station. There was only one problem: her car was blocking me in. I couldn't go anywhere, and I didn't have the key to it. I decided I was committed to this and proceeded to walk to the police station. I walked for over an hour through town. This was interesting, and it wasn't my first time walking through a city. I walked through Baltimore from high school to home on at least two occasions.

I got to the station and asked to see my wife and provided all of the information. They said she was no longer in custody. She made bail. I immediately checked my bank account on my phone. The officer at the desk was not happy with that at all, but I wanted to make sure I didn't just shell out a shitload of money. I was advised to go across the street to the bail bonds office because that is where her bond was made. I departed and headed across the street right away.

I checked in with the guy and he confirmed that bail was

paid in her behalf. She was on the loose. I walked back, with no progress other than some good cardio. I needed to do something. I sat at the house with hardly anything to do. I wanted to go out and do something, but the car trapped me. I went to bed on the couch again, marathoning tv shows. My mind raced with thoughts of what I would say, what would happen, and what would she do? I needed to get out of this house and see people, see things.

The next morning, I decided to call a tow truck company. They were able to take her car and drop it off in front of the house, freeing me up in the driveway. I was given my freedom, and I was ready to use it. Right away I went out to Walmart to buy a few necessities for the house. I completed my shopping and headed home to unload perishables to prepare for my next shopping excursion at the mall. While I was unloading groceries into the fridge, I heard doors slamming outside. Car doors, nonetheless. I went to the door to look. My wife and some dude had gotten into the car and were driving off, followed by my landlord's car, who dropped them off.

I was livid. Who the hell was this dude? I stepped outside as they were pulling away. The landlord had stuck something in the mailbox and pulled off. I went to grab the parcel, and I got a text from her. "Don't bother contacting her, she doesn't love you. You had her arrested and she is staying with me. You are abusive and a piece of shit." That was also the general response I got when I tried to call. Now, for the mail. It was an eviction notice. This one was more fun, it was full of obscenities and insults. It again called me a faggot at least three times and insulted me on a few occasions in the letter. I stowed that away with the last two, envelopes and all.

I realized while paying my phone bill a few days later that Sprint offered a family tracking software on their phones. I clicked the link, and it took me to a Google maps looking view of the area. I clicked my number and it pinged me pretty much at the house. That was spiffy. I clicked her digits next, and it pinged her downtown, right next to the border. I knew where she was. I felt I needed to talk to her, face to face, and find out what the hell we were even doing with each other.

I called my mom and had her on Bluetooth while I drove to the location. She told me I may not like what I see, and it may be best for me to turn around and go back home. I was not about to do that. I went down and found the signal put me at a giant dumpy apartment complex a sneeze from the border. I had no way of telling which one she was in, and I wasn't crazy enough to go beating on the doors. I did the next best crazy thing; I waited in the parking lot for her because I saw her car. I was in the right place.

My mom continued to tell me it may be best to drive off. We made small talk about things, trying to talk about TV shows and whatnot. I suppose that helped a bit. After about a half hour or so, I decided to hit the road. It really was stupid of me to be in this parking lot waiting. What was I expecting to find? So, I backed out of the parking space, and started for the lot exit, when out of nowhere, I see her. She is holding hands with a fat little Mexican dude, whose face looked like he was sucking on a lemon, after smelling a bad fart while staring into the sun. He was wearing Slipknot band merch from head to toe, to include tattoos. I wonder if he likes Slipknot?

I didn't even think. I was already creeping through the parking lot slowly. I threw the door open, the car still in drive, and got out. I don't think they were ready for me. Immediately, I go off with "What the hell is this? Are you banging this dude? Does he know you're married?" She went to her car and grabbed something. "You are nothing to me. We are divorced, asshole!" At that moment, she hit me with the divorce pamphlets. No, I wrote that correctly. The pamphlets.

She threw those generic "Steps to take for divorce" pamphlets at me and assumed that meant we were divorced. She received legal counseling on the process, which meant in her mind, she was in the right to have a relationship. I didn't know what to do. She told her man to get in the car. "Come on Latin Lover, get in. Leave that asshole." He stepped forward toward me. She came over to break it up, whatever was going to go down. I reached out and shook his hand. "Hi, I'm Harry, her husband. Have a great time with her. She's your problem now." With that, I turned and got in my still slowly drifting forward Cavalier and sped off.

I saw in the rear view she tried to run after the car. I don't know what she thought that would solve, but I thought it was funny. I knew I now had to take the ultimate step: Divorce. I had zero ideas about how to even begin. I decided to talk to the JAG office on base. Maybe they could point me in the right directions, offer some sort of help. That is where I headed first thing the very next morning.

I signed into the JAG office and was eventually seen by one of their attorneys. They explained that they cannot help me. It was a conflict of interest, as Mrs. Carpenter is already being represented and aided by the JAG office. What the shit? How is that even possible? They said she came in a few months ago, and because of that, is a client of theirs. That explains the pamphlets she threw at me. As I was leaving, I recognized the same ones on a rack. I needed a lawyer but didn't know where to even begin.

The day was now Christmas Day. I was not a happy camper. Honestly, Christmas was pretty hard for me to put back on track after all of this. I took the decorations down first thing. I had my mom on speakerphone while I did it. I told her Christmas is canceled in this household. Then the most diabolical thing popped into my head. See, her family had been mailing her gifts for the last few weeks. They were under the now disassembled tree. I had an idea to ruin Christmas but without actually doing anything destructive and wrong.

I began to unwrap all of her gifts and calling them out to my mom as I did. I was laughing as I did it because the idea was absurd and hilarious. I unwrapped cookbooks, jewelry, and a bunch of other things. Once I was done, I cleaned up the wrapping paper and neatly stacked all of the gifts on a chair by the door. The idea behind this is simple: I literally took the fun and surprise out of each gift, as well as the means to identify who got you what. This was a victory for me.

She came by later that afternoon. Let me tell you, the real Christmas gift was how much I underestimated her reaction. She broke down crying and had her landlord bestie in tow. "You ruined Christmas, you jerk!" and began collecting her things. I told her "You started it!" and she wiped tears away. "Yeah, well Latin Lover is ten times the man you will ever be! He isn't a giant pussy like you!" She told me that his family has traditions, and she even converted to Mexican to be with him. I'm not sure how that works, but good for you. I assume you get a Baptism in queso dip? I told her I was happy for them, and with that, they hit the road. I decided the following day I wanted to cancel her phone.

I called Sprint first thing in the morning. The lady was very nice, and after I explained the situation she was super helpful. I wanted to cancel her line, which would result in a huge termination charge. I wasn't about that life, but this lady had a better idea. "Do you have an old phone?" Why yes, I do, I have my last model in the bedroom. I retrieved the phone, gave her all of the info, and just like that, her number was linked to this phone. I figured I would just turn it off and just have a spare line for a rainy day and leave it active so she can run back to Verizon with it.

My grandmother called me to see how I was doing shortly

after the Sprint phone call. We started talking for a few and just like that, texts and calls were blowing up that old phone. I told my Grandma what was happening, and what I did. After we hung up, I checked out the phone. It was Latin Lover. Apparently, before Christmas, they had a lover's quarrel over me and the whole situation. She hadn't spoken to him since. That's funny to me and brought my tiny black heart some joy the holiday season.

My sense of humor is what held me together. If not for that, I would have nothing. I listened to the voicemails and read the texts. He begged and pleaded for her. "Please, Mami, oh please come back. I'll change. I'll be whatever you need me to be, Mami, please Mami, please." I couldn't handle it. I was laughing too hard to feel sick or angry at the time. This dude is pitiful, was all I was thinking. I was still very upset over the whole ordeal.

People started coming home from vacation, so I went over Drew and Mallory's place with Erik. I played them the messages, and we all had a laugh. In the span of the few days, he left over fifty voice mails and easily a hundred or two texts, all multi-page messages. I felt bad for the dude. I considered calling him up and buying him a beer for his troubles. He was crying in every voicemail he left. Remember this though: I was the pussy.

I spent New Year's alone as well. Thankfully, I had such good friends and family. They had all called in to check on me. My friends' parents even offered to fly me up to Maryland, so I could be with my friends and family. Unfortunately, it was too late to really take advantage of that, but it was nice to be loved. Work started in a few days so there would be no point in a three-day vacation. My friend K started messaging me on Facebook around 8 or 9 PM. She said she was down to spend New Year's with me in some way because I was not going to be alone. Now, this was the girl that subbed in as Maid of Honor at the wedding, even though to this day my wife was mad about that. Shame about her best friend Feline bailing, otherwise we wouldn't have had to do that. We spent the next two hours messaging back and forth. At 10 PM, she said "Happy New Year!" It was midnight in Maryland, not in Texas. I told her it wasn't midnight, and she even opted to wait until her 2 AM to wish me a Happy New Year. I'm glad I had the support I had with the friends I had made.

The Landlord and I had a few more phone altercations which had nothing to do with rent. She threatened me a few more times that she would shoot me with her pistol she has in her purse all because I'm a bad husband and my wife should leave me, and so on. It got old. I let her go to voicemail from that point on. Work was starting again on January 4th, so I was preparing to go back. I washed uniforms, set up everything and made sure I was squared away. I even made sure my hair was cut and shaved my beard. I was ready to get out of the house with a purpose again.

I went to work, which started at 7, due to it being winter. See, it was balls cold in the early AM. The base decided for soldiers' safety and wellbeing, they would move our PT time to 3 PM. It was warm by then, so it was almost like summer in a way. I always went home in the mornings to change after PT. This was no different for the afternoon either. We finished the work day where I vented to everyone about my struggles, and before we knew it, we were dismissed to change. I headed home in my uniform, parked out in front of my house. It was an in and out deal since I lived almost 20 minutes from work and had an hour to change. I pulled out my key and jammed it into the door. It didn't work.

Ok, maybe it's me and my brain is dead. I retried the key. Thinking there was an issue, I went around back and tried my key there, to no avail. I didn't have time for this. I checked my keys again, and yes, they were mine. Raven's keychain and all. Keys were fine. It's this door that has it out for me. All of the windows had bars on them, so breaking a window and slipping in was out of the cards. I didn't have a clue what to do.

I went back around front to try the front door again. I tried to wiggle the doorknob, maybe it was being dumb. I frustratingly kicked the door with my combat boot a few times and sat down on the steps. I was in the middle of calling Sergeant Ullrich or someone when someone called "Is everything ok sir?" I didn't even look up and continued scanning for the phone number. "Yeah, I'm cool." After a moment, I looked up to notice I was being approached by two officers, hands at the ready on their pistols.

I stood up and set my phone down next to me, hands up. I told them I live here. I'm going to assume either my key is defective, or the locks were changed. The officers demanded proof of residency, which I showed them my ID. They asked who I was calling, and I told them my higher-ups and let them know I can't change my clothes. They became more relaxed the more we talked. I told them a bit of what was going on, the abridged version.

The lady cop looked at me and said "Listen, she is cheating on you and that sounds like she is also unstable. I'd do my best to protect yourself and keep watch on your back. As for the landlord, if you have documents that prove you have the right to be here, contest it." I had no idea the cops could be so much help. This was literally the only good experience I really had with cops.

The male officer chimed in as well. "Dude, go to the courthouse first thing Monday. Go to this floor and speak to this judge. Contest for a writ of entry. That's the best we can do for you. Also, stop by the Victim's Advocate office as well, which is in the State's Attorney office. That's who will be prosecuting her for her court date. Good luck dude." They left on that note and waited in their squad car until I left. I drove over to the 7-11 and parked. I called my Platoon Sergeant to let him know why I wasn't at the formation and also updated Ullrich. There was nothing we could do at this hour. I ended up sleeping in my car. The whole weekend was going to be spent in my car, with one uniform on my back.

On Saturday afternoon, Erik found out everything and offered his barracks room floor. It was totally against the rules, but I was ready to throw down with anyone that had a problem with it. Drew and Mallory loaned out an air mattress, and we hit Walmart to buy a basic grey T and some jeans. I also purchased a large quantity of alcohol of the rum variety, some Captain and some 151. I was about to drown my problems.

Erik and I slammed back shots the whole night. Honestly, it was probably a bad idea, but dammit I needed this. We played the latest Resident Evil on Co-Op, and I tried to get blackout drunk. Erik couldn't handle the 151, and for every shot he had, I had three. He was on the floor pretty quick. I retired to my inflatable bed, only to close my eyes and continue to see the two of them together. I was haunted by images in my brain. I didn't sleep well.

Sunday was spent in recovery. We played some games, tried to sober up, and sort it all out. I think this was the first time life had caught up to me. Locked out of my house. My wife of two years, and technically girlfriend for damn near 10 years, was leaving me in the most uncivil and brutal way possible. At least I had my good looks.

Monday came and I told Ullrich what the plan was. He was well versed in this divorce business, so he knew the deal. He already had me set up my own bank account and only have the required allotment for spouses go to the joint account. I was allowed to run to the courthouse. My first sergeant was also very understanding, and he offered some words of wisdom to me as well. Off to the courthouse, I went.

I made my way up to the judge's office. I filled out all of the required paperwork. The lady at the desk said the process would be that the judge will have to hear both parties and could grant access from there. I thought "Great, this is going to go belly up." I was called into the office. The judge was very nice and inviting. She said to state my case, of why I have the right to be in the home. I explained to her the story and told her I had all of the rental receipts and the agreement in the house. I told her about the deployment, the landlords' insults, and her involvement to help my wife cheat on me.

Apparently, something I said moved the judge. She said "Honestly, Mr. Carpenter, I don't have to hear the other side. Your story was very honest and sincere, and I don't get much of that in here. I will have the bailiff help you with the next steps to gain access. My suggestion to you sir, is you get a storage unit and get the hell out of this mess, and quickly." I appreciated her honesty as well. Everyone could see where this was headed. She signed off on the paperwork and sent me off with the bailiff.

The two of us made small talk on our way to the parking garage. Once we were there, he asked: "So, would you rather her show up with the key, or would you rather me retrieve it from her?" I didn't hesitate with my answer. "I'd prefer you grab it." I didn't want any more interaction with this woman if I could help it. He had the addresses of both the landlord and me, as well as my cell number for any updates. We split ways, and I headed to the house.

I waited at the house for a while. The bailiff ended up calling me on my phone. He said the good news, he would have the key. The bad news, the landlord comes with it. He told me as he was driving over she didn't believe he was a cop, and even called 911 on him and reported an intruder. He was uniformed, showed his badge, the whole nine yards. This family was absolutely bonkers. Except for Noni. I stand by that statement. Otherwise, the whole damn bloodline was nuttier than squirrel turds at the peanut factory.

They showed up, and the landlord let me in. She held onto the key and told me to "Go in and get my shit." The officer stepped in and said "Ma'am, he can actually live here. The judge deemed it in his legal right to be in the residence. If you feel otherwise, you can file a claim to contest and overturn the judgment." She looked offended. "Jesus Christ, this is bullshit." She threw the key at me. She waited on the porch for a while, and the bailiff stuck around until she finally gave up and left. He asked if I needed any other help and took off shortly after I declined. Dude felt bad for me, and I could tell.

CHAPTER 14

No More

I was fed up with this. I needed to get out. I needed to do
it fast. I felt unsafe knowing that at any moment I could
be attacked in my own home. It was a new year, new me. I
felt like my world was changing. I was too wrapped up in this
landlord business to worry about my wife. Honestly, my brain
was more wrapped around moving than it was about my wife
cheating.

I hauled a ton of my belongings to a small storage closet just
outside of the base. I crammed my computer, guitar, amp, and a
ton of other personal belongings in it. I took any and all Army
gear and stashed it in the lockers at work. I tried to get as much
of my personal stuff out as I could. I took the majority of my
clothes and stuffed that storage unit full to capacity. I tried to
apply for an apartment, which I ended up qualifying for. Regardless of my income situation, I made enough money on paper for
it to not be an issue. I did let them know of the issue with my
wife and landlord. They told me I would be evicted if they did
anything, even if I was the victim. After taking some time for
thought, ultimately, the lady at the apartments decided it best I
don't reside there.

The Army wouldn't let me fully have a barracks room since

I was married. I was required to have a house for my family. Trust me, I tried. I had remembered applying for Army housing back when I was in Arizona during training and decided to run that route. I went to their office immediately and spoke with a representative. I told her my wife and I were being run out by a toxic landlord and we need to hurry up with a home right away. I had nowhere else to go. We would be on the street otherwise. The housing lady did some typing on her computer, and there was a home opening up on the 17th. The timing was perfect. It was less than a week away at this point. I was pretty happy about this.

I was told to bring my wife in and sign up for housing the next day. Yeah, sure, bring my wife. Now I'm in a pickle. My name is on the house, but she must sign off as a keyholder, for security reasons. I had to bring her tomorrow. Thankfully, with my quick thinking, I said she went to stay for the week with family and she would be back soon. I was told we could sign when she returns, and the place is ours. Now to find a wife to sign with me.

I asked a coworker to be my wife for a day, and she agreed. We signed on the dotted lines and off we went. The housing was very nice, all things considered. A nice little duplex home. Two-bedroom house. It had a one car garage and a very open floor plan. I was planning to fill it up with my stuff quick. I called Erik right away since he had owned a truck. He and his sergeant both agreed to help me haul things out of the old house. I texted them each the address to the old house and rushed to U-Haul. We were doing the thing.

I picked up the biggest truck I could grab. I am a firm believer in one trip. I didn't have time to return for a second. I needed to just ghost and never be seen at the house again. I pulled up to the house and found Erik and his sergeant ready to go. I popped the truck rear open. "What are we taking?" they asked. "Everything that isn't nailed down. If it's nailed down: find a hammer, un-nail it, and pack the hammer too." We went into the house with a handful of boxes ready to begin. I was grabbing my things in the bathroom and saw in the medicine cabinet; a bottle of Valtrex with my wife's name all over it. I knew exactly what it was for since I watched a ton of late-night television. She obviously wasn't letting her herpes get in the way of her mountain biking or cliff jumping like those people in the commercials.

The two of them went to the den on the opposite side of the house first. They started packing the entertainment center, my CDs, and movies. I was packing the dining room and front living room. Of course, you can already tell what happens next. My wife casually strolled into the front door. I was standing in plain view of my guys who were in the rear den. I was standing directly across the room from my wife. She saw me and right away my wife went from all smiles on her face to a serious expression.

She started screaming for help and to stop hitting her. She threw herself against the wall once or twice. I looked back at the guys, shrugged my shoulders, and returned my gaze to my wife. She started to scream for her aunt, who both she and her husband came rushing in. The Landlord's husband stood in the front doorway. The landlord already had the cops on the phone, screaming at them to come right away. She had called before anything even went down. She tried to tell them I was trying to murder my wife. After she hung up on them, she said, "We got you now you little cocksucker." My wife continued to scream at the top of her lungs. I assume this was in an effort to alert the neighbors or have the cops hurry up.

The part they didn't know, is what was hiding just behind door number three. Two uniformed soldiers stepped out from the den asking what was going on. Immediately my wife stopped thrashing. The landlord's jaw dropped. They were caught red-handed trying to set me up, again. This was the absolute proof I needed to absolve all of those car rides to the police station. I had them this time.

The police showed up, ready for the worst. After getting the lowdown on what happened, especially from a staff sergeant of the United States Army, the cops escorted the landlord out of the house with her husband. They told her she has no right to barge in unannounced. She may own the property, but as a renter, I have full right to privacy. She is supposed to give notice if she is visiting the home for any reason, and I can refuse that visit. I found that interesting and kept that nugget of info for later use. My wife said she came back to the house for clothes. The officers allowed her an escort to get her belongings; a pair of socks, one shoe, and a hat. Those are obviously necessities, you clearly can't live without them. I assumed she already had the one shoe where she was staying, but as it turned out, the other shoe was still in the closet. It was obviously an excuse to be there.

They were escorted off the property. We were told to hurry up and pack and get out of dodge. Remember how I said they left all the furniture in the house and refused to remove it? We took that shit too. We hauled my couch into the truck. We shoved the rest of my furniture, boxes, and belongings into follow. Then we went back for the other furniture that was already in the home before we moved in. I came out ahead with a glass display case, a corner hutch cabinet, end tables, and the coffee table. I packed everything that was in the house. They weren't sure whose was whose, so they grabbed all of the dressers. When I say to grab anything, I really meant it. The house was practically barren, with the exception of the bed. That thing was filthy with god knows how many other dudes.

We drove to the housing unit and I moved in rather quickly. We unloaded everything. Honestly, it may have taken me two days to sort out each room and establish myself. I felt a bit more at ease, but more alone than ever. Everything hit me really hard the first night. I stopped eating entirely. The exception to the rule was once in a while, I'd force myself to Burger King and grab a Double Stacker, because bacon. Yes, back to BK, I know. It was close, just a block away, and it worked. I barely ate my burger when I went, but I needed to be people. I swear that for the next month, I lived off Coca-Cola and rage.

A week or two went by since my move in and everything was going well. I received a court summons. That woman chose to contest my whole writ of entry ordeal. How petty can you be? I needed moral support and a witness, so I asked Erik to tag along. We got permission to go together from our respective squad leaders. The two of us left work for my court hearing. We wore our Army uniforms because we had left work, but I made sure we wore our best ones. It wasn't an arrogance thing, or for leverage, but I'm sure it helped. I had with me the lease agreement, rental receipts, eviction notices, and their envelopes. I was prepared for this day.

We got to the courthouse a little early. We decided we would hang around the cafe food court area and even had breakfast, sort of. While eating, there was a loud thud above us, and on the glass roof. A bird had died and had fallen on the roof. I jokingly said "It's a sign. She's here." We both laughed. Lo and behold, coming through the entrance, was the landlord with husband in tow. We laughed harder at that. Even at my most miserable, I had my humor. It was probably the only thing keeping me from driving my car at a high speed into the mountain.

We went upstairs to the courtroom. I sat in the front row and Erik sat just behind me. The landlord and her husband sat at the far end of the room, away from me. The judge and bailiff came into the room, and it began. She asked what the reason for the contest of writ was on the grounds of. The landlord, without missing a beat said, "Because he is a little cocksucking faggot, that's why. And I see he brought his boyfriend too." Holy balls. This was a courtroom ladies and gentlemen. I maintained my composure, stiff as a board as if I was in a promotion hearing or something. I sat up straight, eyes forward, hands on my thighs.

"That is uncalled for. What is the reason we are here today? What evidence do you have to support your claims?" The judge demanded. The landlord went and turned in a bunch of papers to the bailiff. They looked like the eviction notices I was mailed. After the judge looked at them, I was allowed to view them. They were different. They didn't look like what I had, and I said something about it. We turned in my copies, with post-marked envelopes. That is, except for the last one that was hand delivered. The judge reviewed both sets.

She looked at them hard and good. "Is there a reason this one has the same date as the other written on the letter?" The landlord responded with, "Oh, I must have left that the same. My mistake." The judge read through them thoroughly at this point. "Is there any reason this one is laced with obscenities throughout, as well as threats?" She asked. Speechless, the land-lord responded, "Oh, he must have typed that one up himself." The judge adjusted her glasses and read more. "The post mark-ings do not match any dates you typed. Nor do they match any of the letters you sent. What are you trying to pull here, Ma'am?"

You could feel the tension and anger burning the room up. "That little bastard obviously doctored them up! He knows computers, and I know his little faggot fingers were all over them!" The landlord screamed out. The judge seemed obviously flustered. "One more outburst like that, I'll have you in con-tempt and award Mr. Carpenter his claim immediately. Now, the obscenities seem to match your mouth today. The altered documents in question are the ones you handed to me, both with matching dates. Both with today's date. Care to add any-thing?" The judge sat back in her chair after that verbal smiting.

The landlord was stunned. I was inside my own body gig-gling and screaming but, on the outside, I was like a rock, as was Erik. The judge finally called on him. "What is your purpose here, sir?" He stood up, and clearly and plainly spoke, "I am here as a character witness to both him and that lady over there. She is nuts. We saw it moving him out." That's what did it. That was the trigger to pull to set her on autopilot rage mode. The land-lord stood up and screamed "You two little buttfucking faggots are trying to ruin my good name! I am not going to sit here and deal with this! I should just kick your asses right now!" The judge motioned, and the bailiff hauled her out. Her husband sat quietly in his chair.

The judge asked if I had anything else to present. I turned in the rental receipts, check images from the bank, and the lease. After reviewing the lease, she said it looked like a child had written it. They brought the landlord back in and came to the verdict. "Mr. Carpenter, given the evidence you've presented, and her lack of evidence in addition to her attitude today, I award you this case. Ma'am, please see the clerk out front to pay for your court charges and contempt fee. Thank you." Holy crap! Not only did she have to pay the fee for the court case, but she had to pay for her attitude too! I was also told that the belongings that were already in the house were not docu-mented in the lease, nor was it indicated it was pre-furnished. Everything under the roof was technically mine and she should have had her belongings removed prior to move in if it was not pre-furnished. Also, she was advised in the future she is not to overstep boundaries with her tenants and involve herself in per-sonal affairs and allow that to dictate her business ethics. The landlord was livid. The bailiff came over and expressed his per-sonal feelings of how crazy that woman was to us. Erik and I left as champions. I felt awesome knowing the evil landlord was defeated.

I left the courtroom and returned back to work. However, the fun wasn't over for me just yet. It was early February. I was still not eating, and I was still miserable. I went from around 170 pounds to somewhere around 110 pounds. I felt super unhealthy. I also didn't feel like doing anything about it. My wife had called me around Valentine's Day. She said I owed it to her to treat her to something this holiday since she is my wife. You know, I've done some stupid things in my day. This was one of the top ones. I agreed I would take her out. I have no idea why or how my brain thought it was a good idea. My wife said she stopped seeing Latin Lover, and they weren't talking anymore right now. I set something up on Valentine's Day to meet up somewhere for dinner. The day of, I ended up having to work late and couldn't leave because as you know, it's the Army. I called to let her know the plans were canceled and I felt really bad about it, too. She said in response, "That's ok, Latin Lover is with me and we are already going to a restaurant with his family." She hung up on me. Well, I suppose I learned my lesson right there.

The landlord was waiting in the shadows for her next moment to pounce, as always. Apparently, she called the housing office and reported me as a bad tenant in her free time. My wife was still living in the old house, with Latin Lover no less. The apartment she was staying in with him, his whole family, and three dogs was a tight enough space and was not going to cut it for that many people for much longer. I went down to the housing office and explained to them the situation. Thankfully it was dismissed. She tried to report that my dog poops everywhere and will ruin everything. I had taken the cat with me, so all they knew about was her, and I didn't own a dog. I said it must be their dog and they're trying to pin all of this on me to drag my name through the mud. It was ultimately dismissed, but it wasn't over that easily. Not by a longshot, otherwise, this would be the last paragraph of my story.

I attempted my first shot at filing for a divorce in early March. I had mentally and emotionally come to terms with it and began the process. I found a lawyer across town and saddled up with this guy for the ordeal. I didn't know a thing about lawyers, legal processes, or what was supposed to go down. He said I needed a thousand dollars for the retainer, and I signed on for him as my attorney. My two uncles wired me money to help with the process since they were extremely concerned for my wellbeing. My grandmother also threw in a few bucks to help the process along as well. My family did all they could and put up around 700 dollars toward the retainer. I tossed in the remaining 300, and we were a done deal. I provided the lawyer with all of the information I had, even contact info for my wife so they could track her down to serve her paperwork. I was doing the thing. I was ready.

The second visit was to review the terms of the divorce. I arrived, and I was greeted by a surprise. My ex was sitting in the lawyer's office with the landlord. I had a minor panic attack. He had called her and apparently attempted mediation or reconciliation between us. I couldn't believe it! Did he bring her into the office? He said, "Well, having spoken with your wife I believe there are a few discrepancies with this divorce. I'd like to make a few changes to the process to benefit both parties equally." Wait, you're my damn attorney! Is this how it works? Do they talk to both sides? I asked for my money back since I didn't like the way he did business. He refused. I left the office with no money and no lawyer. The absolute worst part of it was that the divorce process was at a standstill.

Another few weeks went by. I was starting to pull myself together little by little. It was around the middle of March, a few weeks before my birthday once again. Sergeant Ullrich was changing duty stations and leaving the area. At least he got to see closure on that psychopath landlord before taking off. Late one night, I received a phone call. It was the hospital downtown, and they asked for me specifically. "Sir, your wife is in the hospital. She has extremely high blood sugar levels, almost terrifyingly high. Can you please come to the hospital?" I don't know what compelled me to go, but I did. I drove straight to the hospital and checked in at the front desk. I received directions and went to the room she was in. She was passed out. They had her hooked up to IV drips, and she looked pretty bad. The nurse came in to talk to me. I explained to her that I was actually no longer her husband, but I wanted to make sure she was ok. I asked her if Latin Lover, the short Mexican dude wearing excessive Slipknot clothing had shown up. He had not. I provided them with his phone number to call because I was damn sure not calling the dude.

They called him and returned back to me for an update. It was around 1 in the morning at this point, so it was pretty late. Luckily it was a Friday night. The nurse updated me, "Apparently, her boyfriend is at the club right now and can't be bothered to come. He said he will see her when she gets home. I explained to Latin Lover the severity of the situation." Wow, what an assbag. This is the man she left me for? At least I had the common decency to show up, and we were on horrible terms! Eventually, she woke up. She looked at me and was completely confused. "What are you even doing here? Where am I? What happened?" I told her what the nurses told me. She passed out at the mall and was rushed to the hospital with blood sugar turned up to 11. "Where is Latin Lover? Is he on his way?" She said as she was freaking out and sitting up in bed. I shook my head. "No, my dear, Latin Lover is not coming. He is up in the club grinding on other women to be worried about your issues." She got very upset with me and called for the nurse.

The nurse came into the room. My wife asked where her boyfriend was, and why I, her "ex-husband," was even here. The nurse responded, "Well, your emergency contact was Harry. We called your ex-husband, not knowing the circumstances. We apologize for that, but he was very quick to arrive. He did provide us with your boyfriend's contact information and we were able to connect with him." My wife looked unamused. She snapped at the nurse. "Well, where the hell is he? I need my Papi!" By the way, side note here, they called each other Mami and Papi, and it was sickening. Not because of the relationship circumstances, but just because it was thoroughly overused as pet names by them. "Ma'am. Unfortunately, he let us know he was very busy in the club and was "deep in the grind" with some "fine ass ladies", per his statement. Once your blood stabilizes you will be free to go. Mr. Carpenter, are you providing a ride home or shall we coordinate with a vehicle?" I agreed to take her back to the house. Her house. The one we used to rent together. What a pickle to be in.

A few hours later, around 7 or 8, we were discharged. I tossed her in the car, and we started on our way home. It was quiet. No one said anything for the first ten minutes. I finally decided one of us should break the silence and have an adult conversation. "You know, I want you to think about this moment, long and hard. The perfect man you left me for was out with a bunch of ladies grinding at the strip club or something. I spent my entire evening at your bedside to make sure you were ok. Keep that image in your mind for the rest of your days. Not trying to be a dick, just pointing out your decision here." She remained silent as we got on the highway, not even so much as looking at me.

As we were driving down the highway, I passed by a little red sports car. It was Sergeant Ullrich. He saw me in the car with my wife of all people. I thought the man was going to wreck his car or shove his hand through his steering wheel honking at me. I couldn't hear him, but I knew what he was saying. I figured I'd be explaining this one when I got to work on Monday, or even over the phone later today. I know it looked bad. Honestly, it was one of the better things I did. I got to speak my peace and say what I needed to say, in a calm and civil manner. I dropped her off at the house, and she thanked me. She actually said a thank you to me. With that, I drove off. I knew today hit her hard. Latin Lover was in for a hell of a day when he showed back up, that much I could hope for. I never got the chance to explain myself to Ullrich.

Sergeant Ullrich had left to go to a different base across the country. This debacle was now in the court of Sergeant Slaughter. I figured we were all gravy, and I could just continue on with my life and all would be well with the world. It was good, that is until I was called into the office my first sergeant and chief warrant officer. They explained to me that my wife was filing for spousal support, claiming I abandoned her and our unborn son. They know this wasn't true, as everyone was pretty aware of the circumstances I was in. This came as a shocker to me because just a few days before, I sat bedside with her as she almost died. I don't think I could ever get that low on the petty scale to become as petty as she did. They laid out the terms for me. "She will get two-thirds of your income and that will be for her to spend, intended for bills and necessities. But we are smarter than that," The chief said as he began to lay out the details to me.

After the three of us went over the details, I was shaking. Luckily, these two guys knew all about shady women and how to deal with them. "We will put it in an escrow account. If you're confident that it is not your kid, we can handle this. You have deployment orders, that crushes her abandonment case. As for the kid, well, a paternity test will solve that," said the chief. I didn't need all this drama, really, and this was just more added to it. When they finally called to order a full meeting, they had my wife and I in the same room. Of course, the landlord was in attendance, but she was required to wait outside.

I couldn't get away from that crazy woman. "What is it that you need from your husband for support?" The chief asked. "Umm...I don't know," My wife replied. "Well, we are going to need an amount, so throw out a number so we can file the paperwork to get you to sign your statement." "Oh, um. I really don't know." The chief and my first sergeant died a little inside after this interaction. They finally really understood how I felt. The chief got firm with her and said, "Look, we need a number to file for the dollar amount of support. We also need to set up a date in a few months for a paternity test. How far along are you?" She got quiet. Several moments went by in silence. She finally spoke up and asked to step outside for the restroom. She went out and I already knew what was going down. She was conspiring with her terrible life coach in the hallway.

A few moments later, she returned. "I need all that is owed to me. Allot me the maximum support for a spouse in distress." The chief already had a plan up his sleeve, but he wrote in the dollar amount. "Mrs. Carpenter, we will be awarding you, once it is approved, the dollar amount of 5,800 dollars monthly. Does this work for you?" She smiled. "Oh yeah, this works". This was literally my entire housing allotment, in addition to a chunk of my paycheck. How the hell was I going to survive? "Ok, it is a deal. Sign here. Now, in addition to the amount he must pay, you are agreeing to a paternity test to prove that it is, in fact, his child," The first sergeant chimed in. She went completely white as if she saw a ghost. We all knew a bullshitter when we saw one. She nodded. "Ok, it's agreed. The money will filter into a military-controlled escrow account until the paternity test. At which time, contingent upon the results, you will be awarded the sum." Suck it. You won't see a dime, lady. The Army held my money hostage from her instead of putting it in hand. I felt awesome.

Luckily, she got sussed out really quick. It didn't take long for her to crack. She retracted her claims of abandonment since

I had orders to Iraq. She was well aware of my whereabouts for the past year. As for the kid, well, it either didn't exist or it wasn't mine because she gave up the ghost on that real quick as well. The landlord wasn't having any of that. Her aunt coached her to do another thing to me: send me to domestic violence courses. I was reported to the military police once again for domestic violence. This time I was actually at work at the time of the incident, but it didn't stop them from coming to see me. It was decided since I was so abusive that I needed anger management, relationship counseling, and one on one counseling. All at the same time. This was ridiculous.

Taking the classes was an absolute waste of my time. Anger management just pissed me off and made me angry. Relationship counseling was a very one-sided course, considering the other half was never in attendance. My one on ones were maybe the only thing that was remotely useful. One on One counseling basically consisted of me telling all the crazy stories and things I went through, which is more or less what this damn book is doing. I was wasting half of my afternoon in these classes. I had the MPs and El Paso Police called on me more times than I could count throughout March and part of April. It was getting stupid.

One day while up at Walmart shopping, I was loading my trunk up with groceries for myself. I was approached from behind by three Spanish guys. One of them I knew because he was banging my wife. The first one threw a punch in the back of my shoulder blade. I returned fire immediately. I hit one of the guys with a gallon of milk, which went everywhere. My trunk smelled awful for a month. The other guy got nailed by my tire iron for my car jack since I never put anything away. I went swinging wildly as if Mel Gibson told me to swing away because that's just I did. My adrenaline was fired up. They took off. I tossed a few more things into the car and slammed the trunk closed. I went back in to get another milk and to wash up in the bathroom. My wife called that night and said I didn't have to hurt her boyfriend like that. You are seriously holding me accountable for winning the fight because you put a hit out on me?

I recovered from my little attack. Apparently, Walmart didn't get any of it on the security feed. I filed a report, but nothing came of it. One of the many times something didn't go in my favor. I had to regularly attend my classes. They almost consumed my afternoon for the whole week and it was a little obnoxious. One afternoon I wrapped up my anger management class and headed to the house. I got home and noticed my wife's car out front, and my door wide open. How the hell did she get in?

Apparently, the landlord was at it again. She told my wife I was in military housing and they all went to the office. She requested a key from the office, saying she lost hers. They gave her the key and my wife made her way to my house. I walked into the house. Latin Lover walked out of the bedroom with a bag in his hands. I owned a set of display ninja swords, and I pulled one out. "I know her. I DO NOT KNOW YOU. I will end you, sir. Leave my house," I commanded as I brandished the blade. He stepped outside with the bag. The cops showed up shortly, as they always did. The landlord had coordinated the phone call to hit around the time I made it home. The joke was on them, I had Latin Lover removed from the property since his name was not on the house. I couldn't do anything for her, so I played it smart. He waited in the car as she loaded the last bag she could. She only packed about three bags, one of them being my Adidas duffel bag I purchased to take to Basic Training. She also took the cat. I'm still mad about that her taking the cat, and the duffel bag by the way.

The two got in the car and took off, never to be seen again. Or so I hoped. She said she was going to move back to her family, far from me, and Latin Lover was rolling with her. Good riddance. Now I can live in peace, so long as her crazy aunt doesn't start anything. Thankfully, she more or less disappeared off the face of the earth. I could finally focus on Army stuff, myself, and getting my life back together.

CHAPTER 15

Branching Out

I finally decided since things were calming down, I wanted to take a stab at dating. Nothing serious, mainly because on paper I was still considered married, but just to see if I was worth someone's time. I jumped onto two dating websites; Plenty of Fish and OkCupid, because they were free. I was broke and not looking for a subscription payment. I didn't really get any hits for a little while. I assumed it was because I used goofy profile pictures and my description basically described me in a nutshell. No one wanted that. That much was apparent. I was passively looking anyhow, so no harm was done.

I spent most of my time hanging out with army friends like Erik and with my squad mate Freddy. We went on a field trip with Erik trying to get him to be better with the ladies. I assumed it worked in the long run since he's married now. We shopped for a new wardrobe and gave him a slight makeover. We hit the mall. The end result was that Freddy got a few phone numbers and date that evening. I got one or two numbers, and Erik got nothing. None of the numbers I got went anywhere, so I may as well have got nothing too. Even though my life was in a bit of a rut, I was determined to move forward from this.

Sometime in April, I flew home to Maryland to see family

and friends. I had already gone out on several disastrous dates and nothing was working out. I ended up hooking up with this ginger girl who was mutual friends with a lot of my old friends. She was odd. In the end, I really didn't see things working out in the long run. Me and the Ginger hung out most of the time in Maryland. It was nice to just be home for the first time in a long time. It was just comforting to feel actual grass beneath my feet, rain in the air, and seeing green trees once again. I really needed this trip.

Upon my return, I received a court summons. My wife needed to appear in court for that assault charge from way back in December. I immediately had a mild panic attack. Apparently, she had an attorney and was defending against the city, not me. I was requested to be there as a witness if necessary, so I suppose I could sit in the back and hopefully not be bothered. I prepared myself mentally to show up and have to see her once again. It still wrenched my heart each time and it didn't get easier.

Once I was in the courthouse I sat in the back. My wife sat up in front of the judge in the defendant spot. The proceedings began. My wife made a claim with her attorney that I falsified the report, and they have a handwritten letter from me to prove it. For one, if there was anything from me that was hand-written, it wouldn't be admissible in court because it wouldn't be remotely legible. Second, I don't remember writing a letter confessing all of my lies and deceptions. The letter apparently screamed bogus because the judge followed up with "And what reason would your husband have to falsify a report on you?" My wife sat up, very confidently, and said, "Well, he thinks I was cheating on him." The judge looked onward. "Is this Mister Carpenter with you today?" My wife shook her head. "No, this is my boyfriend, Latin Lover, and I love him." The judge shifted in her seat a bit. I couldn't believe what she said either.

The judge recovered from the comment and followed up with the classiest way to bring the truth out of my wife if I ever saw it. "So, how long have you two been together, if you don't mind me asking?" My wife got super proud, perked up and said, "We've been dating for almost a year!" The judge sat back in her chair. "Well, that would imply you are in fact having an extramarital affair with this man, is that not correct?" My wife stood there, dumbfounded. Either she didn't know what the word extramarital meant, or she realized what she had just done. "Is Mister Carpenter in the courtroom today?" I stood up and waved. She dismissed me to sit back down and filed her ruling. My wife was to do community service, substance abuse courses, safe driving courses, as well as counseling. Holy cow, is this what it feels like to be on the other side of that? What a feeling it was. I guess she was able to complete those things back in Maryland apparently, so she left the city once the court session was over.

I felt a sense of relief that something was done. I can't begin to tell you how great it was. My next step on the to-do list: I needed to find a lawyer to start this divorce process. It was May, and the weather was fantastic. I would get out of work and make my way to the latest attorney of the day. I bounced through so many offices. I was already pissed and still mad about the first one taking my money, and the state bar was still not doing a damn thing about it. Apparently, he was allowed to jump ship, take my money and work with my wife. So obviously, I was super wary of setting up a new one.

I went to the first lawyer. This lady immediately asked me what did I do wrong? That really is not a way to start any client relationship, is it? If I'm looking to hire you, why am I being looked at like I'm the guilty party? I told her the brief backstory and asked what the next steps would be. She said "Well, you should probably assess how much you have in assets and prepare to divide them. It would be the best way." I didn't like what I heard at all. If I wasn't the problem, why should I essentially buy off my wife? She had a lot of her belongings still at the house. Apparently, she left behind quite a lot of things. I left that lawyer and did not return.

I went on a few more dates and met some very nice people. I actually remained friends with one of the girls, even though I probably wrecked that chance by being awkward and still emotionally damaged. I'll take the responsibility on that one. It was totally my fault. At least she's cool people and she's a good long-distance friend. The ginger at this point still talked to me occasionally over the phone. I was still working on bettering myself. I had a lot going on, not to mention I still needed a decent lawyer. Life was rough.

Work was the only place that I really didn't have issues. Everyone was chill, and I got along with my team. Sergeant Slaughter was pretty awesome and really knew how to drive morale home. We'd spend an extended lunch together on Tuesday, properly dubbed "Team Build Tuesday." We also went out for training adventures on Thursdays. These were our designated training times, and at one point we landed a tour of a NASA facility by sheer accident. We lucked out and saw a massive plane called the Super Guppy. We wandered into the building, and the tour guide ran from the back room and yelled, "You guys here for the Super Guppy Tour?" We smiled and nodded. That was one of a few great times I had while serving. The Army was the only place things were going right. I was injured, but I pushed through it. They tried to get me to do adjusted fitness and walk. I hated it because the injury walk was more painful than actually running. You had to walk three miles in thirty minutes and swish your hips in order to make the right pace, which killed my hip. At least with running I could push off with my right leg harder and get some air and distance.

At one point in the early summer, we started doing training at New Mexico State University. It was just some job training that Slaughter managed to snag for us. It was a solid excuse to be out of work. New Mexico didn't look all that different from El Paso, except it was a little flatter, with fewer high-rise buildings. The content we learned was actually interesting. Currently, I was talking to a few girls on dating websites. There was some girl in my unit, who worked upstairs in the same building. There was some girl who worked at a bank who lived in New Mexico and some other girl who was a chef at a restaurant, also in New Mexico. Oh, there was also some girl who wanted to go out on a date. She said it was her birthday, and I better bring a gift no less than 50 bucks, and the restaurant bill was to be no less than 100. Well, I bid you a fond farewell lady, before we get this ball rolling.

The two girls in New Mexico I could never land time to actually go out on a date with. Both were extremely busy with work, so we could never really get a free second. They were also terribly unresponsive to messages, so I started to drift away from them. I tried to focus more on this girl at work, who was obviously closer and much more convenient. We had never met in person. on one occasion at work, we had the chance. She came down to do some work in my office. I sort of hovered around without blowing my cover that she was talking to me online. She talked about drugs, partying, and other crazy things. I dodged a bullet and moved on from that, but it also meant I really didn't have any prospects.

Weeks later, I finally got a response back from the bank girl. We chatted for a few moments, but then, as before, it died off. The other girl at least said there was no chance. She was far too busy with school, working two jobs, and life to maintain any kind of relationship. I respected that honesty. I found a second attorney sometime in June. He literally had no spine. His methodology of dealing with my wife was, "give her what she wants, and she will leave you alone." I really didn't like this guy and walked out of his office. Is this what all lawyers were like? I had no idea what I was doing, but I'm sure I was doing it wrong.

I ended up going on a date with a girl who I mentioned earlier on, where I botched it but remained friends. Honestly, she was probably out of my league, or it was my head getting in the way again, as it always did. We had set up to meet at the movies to see the Pirates of the Caribbean movie together at the end of the week. I was pretty excited. She messaged me, and like an idiot, I was like, "hot girls don't message me. Is your computer broken?" Obviously, I've never been good with women, and that wasn't about to change now. She still agreed to this date. I also had the ginger back in Maryland constantly chatting with me, but she had a lot of issues she needed to work out.

I went on the date, and her friends went with us. No biggie, I didn't see this date going anywhere anyhow, but at least her friends were pretty cool. The movie was pretty fun, and if I remember right, I held her hand in the movie. We went off to grab some ice cream afterward. She got in her friend's car and drove off home. I figured that was about it, and we were done. I gained a major confidence booster, since the majority of the girls I had dated previously were unkempt, batshit crazy, or just really crappy people. This was a nice change of pace, and I was doing pretty well.

A few days after the movie date, I received a phone call from a Pennsylvania number. It was my wife, and she wanted to talk. She started by making small talk, but I wasn't really in the mood. She cut right to the chase and posed her proposition. "So, you know how you have the house, right?" Yeah. "Well, it's two bedrooms, so I was thinking. We wouldn't have to divorce. Me and Latin Lover could live in the back bedroom, and you could keep the main bedroom. You could have me any time you wanted in return and do whatever you want to my body. We could all live together in the same house. Would that work for you?" Was she actually serious right now? Am I being Punked? Where is Ashton? This could not be for real. I didn't really know how to respond.

I was quiet for a few moments. I took a moment and collected myself because I was still shocked someone would have the audacity to propose this kind of idea. I finally responded. "No. Not really. Doesn't sound like a fair deal. It actually sounds pretty messed up." She got defensive immediately. "Wow. Here I am going out on a limb, willing to sacrifice myself to make you happy, and you shit all on me." Is this now my fault? I was more dumbfounded and angrier than any other emotion. "Wow. So, you assume I want you back so damn bad, that I'll sacrifice my dignity, let you and your boyfriend cozy up in my house, and I screw you as I please? Where in your brain did that rattle around in the empty space and sound like a good idea?" I went off on her. She was pissed. "You will never have someone as good as me. NEVER!" She screamed. The fight was starting to escalate. I told her "Well, sure I will. I'm actually dating someone right now. This girl is Hispanic, a model, and much better than you'll ever be." She was livid at those remarks.

She was actually serious about her proposition. "You're dating someone? So, you're cheating on me? I'll have you in jail for this," she scoffed. Well, for one, they don't throw you in jail for it or you'd have been there long ago. Secondly, it's documented in court that you were having an affair long before this whole thing even played out. Good luck. I raised my voice for the final time over the phone. I partially regret what I said, but I also don't. "You enjoy all your damn boyfriends all over the world. I hope Latin Lover knows what he is getting into with you sleeping around with anything that has a dick. I hope you get AIDS and die!" And with that, I hung up the phone. I felt that was a high note for me, in a way.

Weeks later, the Ginger sprang a surprise visit on me. She scheduled a trip for two whole weeks and planned to stay at my house. She got my address from forwarding my football jersey she stole from me, Matt Stover, which was the greatest Raven's kicker of our time. Yes, I owned a kicker jersey. While she was down, she was distant. She slept on the couch, didn't really talk to me, and at one point, she invited every phone contact over for a cookout. That was interesting, scrambling to figure out food and drinks once the first guest showed up and told me about the text. A day or two later, she sat on my front sidewalk and colored with the neighbor kids chalk. This was not a fun adventure for me by any means. My neighbor even said, at a later time, that she introduced herself as my "booty call" even though there was barely any booty had. Thank god she shipped back to Maryland and stayed there.

I did go on a follow-up date with the girl from the movie date. After eating dinner, we drove around looking for nightclubs that night. One of her friends was underage, so we ended up hanging out at her house for a bit. Ultimately, it didn't work out. Initially I took it the wrong way, but in the end, it was me and my stupidity. I was pissed though, regardless of who's fault it was. The following day while heading to NMSU for our classes, I brought it all up in conversation. I was telling Rob, my drinking buddy from training and one of my oldest relationships in the Army, all about my troubles. I said that it's ridiculous that people could be so shallow and that I'm already filtered by my looks I assumed. I can't get a decent woman to give me the time of day. The only ones that do are totally crazy, have something severely wrong with them, or are just nuts. I decided at that moment I was messaging Banker Girl.

I hit her up on the dating app messenger. In person, I was hostile, angry, and bitter. I sent the message, "What are you doing? Do you want to go out at all?" After the messages sent, we went to class. This girl had like four photos. She looked good, but she had a very empty profile. Her interests were "Concerts, and that is all." I had no idea who or what the hell I was getting into. At least I knew she had a job, which was more than some of these other girls. Once we finished the class I checked my phone. I did indeed have a message waiting for me. She said it was a rough day and needed to get out and do something. I offered to meet her back in New Mexico after we drove back to base. The drive was almost an hour each way, but I was willing to do it. She responded a few moments later, as we were driving the van back to base. She said she would meet me in El Paso around 6. That gave me enough time to get home, shower, and prepare for my date. We were meeting at The Olive Garden located just in front of the mall.

I drove my car over with plenty of time to spare. I parked and went to get a table for two. They asked if the entire party was available and I told them we weren't. It was ten after six, and I didn't know where bank girl was, nor did I get a message. I waited patiently in the seating area up front. Finally, a text message came through. "I think I went to the wrong Olive Garden. I'm coming to the right one now, see you soon." Well at least I wasn't being stood up yet, that was a plus. About fifteen minutes go by, and she still isn't there. Well, there you have it, ladies and gentlemen, stood up. The story of my life. I felt a vibration in my back pocket. I got a text shortly after the hostess checked on me yet again. The text read, "Ok, I'm not coming inside. Sorry." What? Wait? Not coming inside? Great. She must have seen me, was instantly repulsed and sped off through the highway.

I decided to respond back and ask her why not. She said she didn't want to text why, just meet her in the parking lot, by the silver Lancer. I didn't know cars, nor did I know what the hell a Lancer was or remotely what it looked like, but damn if I didn't go looking. I found her in the parking lot, door ajar, fanning her back off. She said she was super embarrassed. Her seat covers caused her back to sweat really bad since it was so hot out. There was a massive sweat stain on the back of her shirt. I thought that was hilarious because here I thought it was me, but it turns out to be some hot weather and a furry seat cover.

We went in and had dinner. I ordered unlimited Soup and Salad as I always do. She wanted to order something small, so she ordered a pizza. Who orders a pizza at Olive Garden? We made small talk, mostly about work, music, and our interests. She seemed nervous to talk to me because she was bouncing her leg with her other leg crossed over it. She kept kicking the table. We talked about the meet and greet tales of famous people, and I told her about the time Vanilla Ice ate my French fries. We talked for hours. It was the most relaxed time I ever had. I looked up and noticed we were the only two in the restaurant, and the staff had already cleaned up. They were nice enough to let us keep talking. We were respectful, and I paid the bill and we left. We stood in the parking lot for another hour, easily. She was tall, which was my first observation now that we had a moment to think about that. She even made the comment, that she can't be taller than someone she dates, and currently, she was. She took off her heels and was luckily just a few inches shorter than me.

We talked more outside our cars, as two of the only vehicles really in the parking lot. At some point, I believe around 1 AM, the security guard for the mall came by and told us kids to go home and stop causing trouble for him. We giggled and parted ways. I assumed that was that. She got a meal and was never talking to me again. I went to work and talked her up to everyone. I thought the date went very well. It was nice to be with someone that isn't totally bonkers for a change. It's a shame there wasn't going to be a follow-up date. I went on with my training at NMSU with Sergeant Slaughter and crew and went about my business. Late one day I got a message. Bank Girl said she wanted to hang out again. I offered for her to come over my house. I would make dinner, and we could watch some movies. She agreed, and I was honestly shocked. She also sent me her phone number, and I sent her mine. It was much easier to do that as opposed to hoping the dating app messenger loaded right. I had a date night to look forward to after work, and thankfully it was Friday. Our first date was on Tuesday.

I prepared some chicken breasts and a few sides. I went all out and cleaned the entire house more than it ever had been before. I showered, changed, and was ready for the night. She came over at six. We ate dinner, which she said was really good. Thank god, because, for most of my relationship I was told I was an awful cook. That was because my wife swore she was Rachael Ray Junior and was going to have a cooking show one day. That's also the reason I despise that woman, her show, her merchandise, and her voice. Nothing personal, Rachael.

After we ate the food, I cleared the plates and offered movies. I didn't have too many movies but thank god for Netflix. We started the night with Zombieland, her choice. Already an awesome start to the movie night. We followed it up with the first GI Joe. At some point, she made a joke about the two guys in the movie fighting saying, "They only fight because they're mad their pee-pees are small." What was that about? I cracked up. That's some off the wall crap I'd say. We tried to watch some South Park, but she ended up starting to fall asleep while laying across me. At first, she had her head resting on her hand. I told her she was going to wake up in pain if she stayed like that. She didn't care, but she nodded off anyway. Shortly after another episode, she woke up with a hand cramp. I said, "I told you so that it was going to hurt." I even made an offer for her to move to the bed if she was going to sleep. She declined, readjusted and fell fast asleep. I didn't move an inch.

I must have been in the same upright uncomfortable position for hours. I suffered through it all. Honestly, I wasn't moving because a hot girl fell asleep on me and that was a rare occurrence. I was sitting upright, and not even in range to rest my head against the wall or back of the couch. I had fallen asleep in some strange places while in the Army such as lockers, piles of rocks, and storage totes, so I managed. She woke up at daybreak and apologized for staying over because she hadn't meant for this to happen. She grabbed her things and left. Well, there goes that one, but it was fun while it lasted.

I was feeling a lot more confident with myself, which was a change for the best in my behavior. I started actually caring about myself and my wellbeing. Banker Girl, however, dropped off again for the next week or so, but I was sort of ok with that I suppose. I even felt good enough to break it off with any of the girls I was seeing or conversing with online. I had to tell the ginger to scram once again because she was insistent that we were going to be married, have babies and live in a faraway castle somewhere. Thank god I dodged that bullet when I did.

I received a text finally about a week or so later, sometime in the middle of August. It was the Banker Girl, and she was apparently wanting to get back together to do something. We had more training to do up her neck of the woods, so I drove myself up to the school and departed from my team afterward and met Banker Girl at a pizza place. We grabbed some nice, amazing pizza. We talked about partying, our dumb pasts, and vomiting from drinking too much. I'm so glad that someone in this world was able to share in such captivating tales of barf while sharing a pizza. After pizza, she asked if I wanted to meet her family because they were going camping next weekend. Now, I was in an Army unit that went to the field on a routine basis. I did not want to go camping for either work nor fun. I liked this girl, so I decided it was best to put that thought aside and agreed to meet her family for this camping adventure.

We were going out to a place called Ruidoso, located in New Mexico. It was about three hours away, and I had never really driven that far since I had been in El Paso. Not that far at least, since me and my wife met the late comedian Ralphie May when he performed at the Dallas Improv. This was a long haul because I didn't know what this place was or was going to be. At least with Dallas, I understood it was a city and they drew it pretty well in that show King of the Hill. I had an understanding of East Texas. This new place, Ruidoso, it was an absolute mystery.

We drove through the middle of nowhere. We passed through White Sands Missile Range, which was a whole lot of nothing apart from it having bright white sands; like being at a beach with no water. We drove through a tiny town called Tularosa, which was a one-horse town, but I didn't even see the horse. We stopped at a little diner on the highway in Tularosa for some authentic Mexican food. Now, I knew nothing about "authentic" Mexican food. My knowledge was limited to Taco Bell, that Chico's Tacos place and a now-defunct restaurant back in Maryland called Chi-Chi's. My date, however, was Hispanic and took the reins and we ordered food.

So, after finishing our food, we started back towards the car. I should clarify; after I finished picking at my food and avoiding the beans and other things I didn't trust, we started toward the car. They actually had a giant pay phone booth outside. I cracked a joke about Rufus showing up for tacos, or that I actually discovered the Payphone that Adam Levine was trying to call with all of his change. She shook her head at my dumb joke, which was an improvement over being called an asshole or childish idiot by my wife.

Actually, this was an entirely different experience altogether. It's not that I didn't have good times with my wife. It's that there were so many bad times, they snuffed the life out of the good ones. We went on trips to the Aquarium, the Zoo, and did things that couples do, except usually they would end in a blowout fight. Even when we were dating, everyone only really saw the tonsil hockey smooching couple at school. The veil was never lifted with the issues that went on behind the scenes. This experience, this was different. The good times, few as they were, felt genuine. Even dating the other girls, aside from one who I dated for over a month or so, felt empty and that they were dead ends.

We made our way to Ruidoso. I knew we were getting close only because the terrain went from an empty desolate desert full of nothingness to a beautiful wooded, grassy mountain range. There were log cabin buildings everywhere. There were a lot of strong Native American roots in this town. It also dropped almost twenty degrees in temperature going in. I had the windows open, enjoying the clean, crisp, not sandy air. This was a pretty kickass place, and I was glad she took me. I honestly didn't even know there was a beautiful area in such close proximity to where I lived, because I assumed it was all sand and dirt. We were on the way to a campground just beyond the town, near a massive lake.

We were driving down the dirt roads and were greeted by signs, which actually helped direct us closer to where her family was at. Some other family had been having a family reunion, and there were "Garcia Family Reunion" signs posted all over. Considering I was in the Army with at least 17 Garcia's, I assumed this was the equivalent of Smith for the Hispanic community. I could imagine whoever they were, it was an amazing party. We found our way to the campsite, and everyone had their RV's parked. This was new, RV? Not a tent? We pulled in and joined everyone by the campfire. I met her cousins, aunts, parents, Granny, and a few other members of her family. There were a bunch of people here, and it was a lot to take in. They all seemed nice, and we sat by the fire and got to know each other. Banker Girl started to feel tired since we were both up very early and did a lot of driving. She said she was about to head to bed. It was just starting to be sunset. I joined her since I didn't know these people much, and I wasn't about to be left alone.

Her cousin said we could bunk up in his RV since he had two beds. Two beds? These things are amazing! I went inside, and sure enough, at each end of the RV, there were beds. The two of us began to bed down for the night. I was freezing outside since my dumb ass self wore shorts and a T-shirt. I wasn't aware we were driving to the Arctic. I climbed under the sheets with my shorts and shirt on. She asked if I was really wearing all of my clothes to bed. It's not like I packed my Ninja Turtle pajamas or something, so, yeah. After taking the subtle hint, which I never really did in the past, I ditched the shorts and shirt. I still had my socks on, since that was how I rolled.

She ditched her clothes and was down to bra and panties. She was gorgeous. She climbed into the bed with me, and little spooned me. Holy cow, her family is right outside, they're not going to be mad? Her dad isn't going to come in and fight me in a few moments? I had been so conditioned to this behavior for so long, I was constantly on guard. My wife's dad tried to get physical for kissing his daughter in the upstairs of their big ass house and would scream "No Hanky Panky" constantly, even until we were in our twenties. Tonight, nothing happened. No one came in. This was new. This was nice.

We made small talk while we laid there. We talked about some rapper chick riding an elephant in the club, which I clarified was about drugs. I came from the hood and apparently, she did not. We talked about a bunch of stuff and must have chatted for hours. Her family laughed and carried on outside while we talked. At this hour? Holy cow! Go to bed people. I checked my phone, and it was 9 PM. Clearly, neither were tired, but we retired to the beds anyway just to be close. I wasn't complaining.

A few hours later while we were asleep, Banker Girl got up

out of the bed. She threw pants and a shirt on and needed to use the restroom. The RV we were in wasn't set up for that, but the other one across the way was. She struggled with the screen door and yelled out, "I swear to God I will pee out this door! Work dammit! Let me free!" The door eventually opened. That was the funniest thing I had seen and heard. She came back in, and soon, everyone went to bed. I thought it was hilarious how she was, and I hoped this would actually work out. I also hoped her family wasn't going to murder me at some point in the woods.

The next morning, we all woke up early. I was usually early to rise since the Army made me that way, but everyone else was already up before me. Her Granny had made Enchiladas the night before, and I picked at them. They were good, but I still didn't get into much Mexican food. In the morning, her dad was making breakfast. Finally, something normal to eat out here. Something I understood. We had French Toast, among a few other things, and chatted for the morning. One kid was walking around holding a worm yelling "I got a worm!" Banker Girl responded to him, very deadpan "That's nice kid." I don't know why that was so funny to me. The same kid also ran around yelling "What the hell!?" The kid yelled this the whole time too, which was cracking me up.

We returned back to civilization later that day after some shopping and a stop at the casino. Casinos were pretty popular out this way since there was a lot of Native American reservation territory up here. We got home and eventually parted ways. I headed back to El Paso. I had an amazing time and honestly enjoyed camping for the first time in a very long time. I made a mental note to pack better if we ever return. Pants and jacket would be an absolute must, even if it was the middle of the summer.

Life was going very well. My Army career seemed to be

doing well also! Sergeant Slaughter and the rest of the crew were all great to work with, and we were doing great things by slipping off to training all the time. What a time to be alive. Everyone noticed a major change in my attitude, too. I was no longer just moping around, being miserable. In the past few weeks, I was cheerful, optimistic, and overall a blast to be around again. I hadn't been this way in some time, and it was actually kind of nice. Officially, Banker Girl and I labeled each other as Boyfriend and Girlfriend. I still had a roadblock in the way. I needed to get divorced before I made this public, like on Facebook and stuff.

CHAPTER 16

You Don't Gotta Go Home, But You Can't Stay With Me

I really had to buckle down and get rid of my wife, but with the lawyers in town being absolute garbage, where I was I to turn? I couldn't get help from the Jag office on post since they technically "represented" my wife, so I had to do my own digging. I found an attorney who was moments from my old house with the crazy aunt, so I ventured up to check this guy out. One of the perks of being in the Army, I got to dip out and go take care of all of this business because they wanted it over with too.

I drove out to this office complex and parked out front. It was in a strange location, not like the last few which were located in business parks and huge buildings. This was a small building, butted up against some cleaners or flooring company. I went inside and spoke to the lady at the desk. I told her that I was looking to divorce my wife and filled her in on the back-story, as much as they needed to hear with an abridged version. She said she would get me in with the attorney right away and went into his office to talk to him. Moments later, they were calling me into the office. I had already had terrible experiences with the last few that I visited, so I already went into this guy's office with a predetermined mindset that he was about to screw me over.

I sat down in the big squishy leather chair. He looked up from a case file he was working on, typed a few last-minute words on his computer. He swirled around to look at me. He folded his hands on his desk and gave me his undivided attention. "Mr. Carpenter, you are here to seek counsel with divorce proceedings. Is that correct?" I nodded my head. He typed a few things into his computer and jotted a thing down on a notepad. "Ok, well, let's talk business then," he said as he moved away from his computer screen. I was ready for him to slam me with his fee and how I need to just turn my butt up and let her do what she wishes to me once again. "Let's talk about what terms we are laying down. To put it simple sir, 'What do YOU want out of this divorce?'" I had never been asked that. He cared about my needs and what was actually in my best interest. I became Phillip J. Fry and was ready to wave a stack of money around at him. I kept it simple for him. I wanted my stuff to be mine and her stuff to be hers. I let him know about the car she has with my name on it, and he agreed that we should do something about that and would look into what could be done. After we laid everything out, of course, the money was discussed.

Of the three or four attorneys I had interacted with, this guy was by far the best. And this is to include the one my wife hired for her assault case. However, money was an issue. It was damn near 1500 bucks to make her go away. After everything we had discussed, we decided the fully contested divorce is what we should prepare for, given her mentality and the company she kept. I didn't have that to just dump on the table, but this guy worked with me. We decided that I would pay 250 bucks each paycheck, which worked out to a paycheck coming twice a month. At that rate, we should be paid off pretty quickly. He said I should come back in a week after he has had the time to draw up the initial paperwork, and that I should be prepared to make the first payment then. Since it was the start of September, that worked peachy for me. I left the office with the best feeling I had my body since I ate a gallon of ice cream and watched Armageddon in my underwear. I kid, this was actually leaps and bounds better.

I went through the next week in a haze. I was going to do the thing. I needed to do the thing. My wife had been running around on me for years starting with the one that I can now confirm with Joseph, the dead cat dude she stayed with those two nights. I'm sure it went on before that, but that was the first encounter and I still stuck through it. I shoved my head in the sand and pretended everything was ok, sitting through at least four more guys that I could confirm at this time. I needed to do this, my mind needed it. Payday finally came, and I left work early to rush over to the lawyer's office. I told the lady at the desk I was ready to pay, but she told me to at least hear what the lawyer had to say and review the documents first. That sounded like a better idea.

I went into the attorney's office. We went line by line. In short, it detailed that my property was mine and hers was hers since she already came and grabbed a chunk of it. There was so much left at my house though, stashed in the garage. I asked him about that property. If I clearly had her possessions, do I need to distribute them? He said if I could prove she took a handful of her belongings, then she already took her half. Luckily, a police report was available for that date because she called them, so we were square on that. As for the car, he worked in a legal blurb that stated she needed to refinance and change ownership of the vehicle to remove my name from all documentation, within 60 days. Unlike Maryland, Texas was a state that allowed me to file for a divorce without issue. In Maryland, there is a year cool down period and a huge battle that I'm sure she would have to drag out. Texas was a no contest state, and whether or not she agreed to it, we would be divorced. I liked how this played out as time went on.

After reviewing the entire document and clearing up any questions I had, we agreed to go forward with it. He said the documents would be sent out. Whether she returns a signature agreeing to it or not, we would still go to court in late October and finalize the divorce. Holy cow! Pinch me because it sounds like I am coming out on top! I went to the front desk, paid the nice lady, and went on my way. A happy ending to a tragic story. We weren't over yet, not by a long shot. If you actually thought I found a nice girl, destroyed the evil ex in court, and lived happily ever after, at this point, then you either gotta be crazy or have ignored the last several chapters of this book.

Bank girl invited me up to a thing called "The Enchilada Festival" in New Mexico. I've been to chili cookoffs, but never an entire festival dedicated to burritos covered in sauce. I agreed, and we went out. It was basically a giant fair where they cook the world record holding giant enchilada. I was enjoying everything they had to offer; live music, games, and amazing food. We finished up our date night and headed back to her place. Her parents were waiting for us when we got in. I was thinking that we were in trouble or something, even though we were grown adults in our mid-twenties. "Can you come to join your father and I out on the back patio by the fire? Harry too." Uh oh, this does not sound good. We hesitantly followed them out to the back yard.

They started to give a speech about relationships and how they sometimes go through rough times. Her parents started to go on about how sometimes they don't last, and it is best to move on from one another. Holy crap, was I witness to the "talk" about divorce? This was probably why I needed to stick around, to be a shoulder to cry on or something once the conversation ended. We never did make it to the end of the conversation, as my phone rang. It was my ex. I don't know why I answered or what compelled me to actually hold the conversation out back. I stepped off to the side and I tried to keep the conversation private. Unfortunately, my voice projects and she yelled loud enough half of the west coast could hear her.

"What do you mean we are getting a divorce? Are you crazy?" She must have just received the divorce papers. I continued to get belittled for a few more moments by her over the phone. "So why the hell do you think you can just divorce me?" I composed myself, and said, "Is Latin Lover next to you in bed?" "Well, yeah. He is. Why?" I smiled. "That is the reason I'm divorcing you. You're a cheater, a liar, and a terrible person. And you can't cook." We continued the argument for a few more moments before I hung up on her and turned off my phone. I walked back to the fire pit to join her family, who was dead silent. They stopped their conversation and were watching me the whole time. Her dad took a sip of his beer and looked me dead in my eye sockets and said, "You're married?"

Awkward doesn't begin to describe the feelings in that backyard. Her mom spoke up. "Yes, he told me he was divorcing. He was telling me the other day when he stopped by to pick our daughter up." "You knew and didn't tell me?" He was livid. I left shortly after in my little car, and things were fairly tense between me and her dad. I figured that was the end of the relationship since her dad was probably going to destroy me with his brain using rage powers. Thanks for calling when you did. You managed to get the last laugh and ruin my life once more if you're reading this.

As it turned out, it wasn't the end of the world. I was invited back over and got to join my girlfriend for dinner and a trip to the mall. I went back to her house and talked with her parents since the initial shock of the news had settled. The tension was a little less and was reduced after the situation was explained. It's not that I was a two-timing guy trying to play their daughter while I had a family. I had actually tried to get out of this situation the past year. Once the fires were out at her house, I continued to pay toward my divorce with the lawyer to keep that train rolling.

I had a guy at work get me into comic cons and cosplay around this time as well. We were going to El Paso Comic Con, which was my first foray into the nerdy world I now find myself in. Bank girl flew to Florida because it turns out she was born and raised there, and all of her friends were there. In her absence, I went to the convention. I went dressed as a terrible Green Lantern with a bright green lit suit that didn't fit. I know how Ryan Reynolds feels now since that was his first major Superhero. It was also mine until I took up the mantle of dressing as Deadpool. They were some dark times for both of us. I enjoyed myself and found it got me through a lot of my divorce woes.

On one visit to the lawyer in October, I went in to pay the lawyer as I always did. The lady behind the desk and I had talked about my comic convention fun, my costumes, and thought it was great that I actually found a nice girl. This visit was different. She told me she had received phone calls from my ex constantly. She would beg and plead for them to undo the divorce and tell me to not do it because she loves me. She never meant to hurt me, and it was all a big misunderstanding. They advised her on multiple calls that they cannot disclose information, nor can they stop the divorce since she was not represented by them. They also advised she seek legal counsel if she needed further help with the divorce. She asked if they could represent her, and of course, was denied immediately. I couldn't believe the stories this lady was telling me. My ex was calling and harassing my lawyer's office?

I was about to pay the bill when a phone call came through. I told her I was cool to wait since I just left out of work. She can take her time because I had plenty. She picked up the phone and greeted the way she did on all phone calls. "Hello, law office, how can I help you?" I always hated that because I never knew if I called the right office when I called in. Doctors do that, and so do dentists. It drives me crazy. After a few seconds on the phone, she looked at me and pointed at the phone and mouthed out "It's Her." I couldn't believe it. She was calling while I was in the building. The legal aid told her what I assume was the usual routine at this point, "No, Mrs. Carpenter, we cannot cancel the divorce. No, we cannot tell him we are not servicing him anymore. No, we will not tear up the divorce paperwork. Have a nice day. If you would like to contest, you may appear at the hearing which is disclosed on the divorce documents." With that, the phone was hung up. She looked at me and said "How did you deal with that for so long? She always calls, usually right after you leave. This was the first one she's done before or while you were here." We laughed about it for a while because it was so crazy.

I tried to be the bigger person as often as I could. I started going through the possessions in the garage to see if there was anything worth saving or if it was all trash. I found all kinds of things like clothing, purses, shoes, makeup, as well as the lotions and other soaps she was trying to sell in another one of her Pyramid scheme companies. Nothing much of value, but then after some digging, I found things. Baby books, old photos, VHS tapes of plays and graduations, a jar of baby teeth. All kinds of keepsake items. I called her on the phone and told her what I had found in addition to her possessions. I offered to get a storage unit nearby, or one within reasonable driving distance of her choice, and stash everything of hers to retrieve at a later time. She would just have to foot the bill. It seemed like a reasonable thing to do at the time. I was told I could shove all of the stuff up my ass and die, and she disconnected the phone.

I tried my hardest to salvage this. I knew baby books and

tapes are one of a kind, and I doubt they had a room full of backups. I called her grandmother, who told me basically the same thing. I got the same thing with mom, and I got a death threat from dad. Well, that settles it. I'm not being a good guy. I did my best. It was a Saturday around 10 or so, and I prepared to start throwing things away in the trash. I opened the garage door and started throwing away pounds of makeup. A few Spanish people came over and said, "Yard Sale?" It hit me. There was a yard sale going on around the block. I told the lady, "Yes, give me a moment," and threw a blanket over my car hood. I was setting shoes out, clothing on a rolling closet rack I had in the garage, and there was an army of people coming to look. I was throwing purses on the ground after checking all of the pockets and compartments for personal info or money. I couldn't move fast enough. I must have tossed twenty or thirty purses and dozens of pairs of shoes onto my driveway and car. I pulled out the soaps and lotions she was selling too. The first lady held up a purse and asked how much. "Uh, fifty cents." She looked like she saw a ghost. She looked back at the purse and back at me. "Misser, this Prada," in her broken accent, still in shock. I looked up at her and said "Oh, jeez. I didn't even catch that, sorry. One dollar." I almost killed a Spanish lady in my driveway. Her heart must have skipped several beats and was legally dead for a moment. She finally reacted and started digging through everything.

Eventually, I had a handful of people digging through everything in the garage. There was no going back. I gave the chance for my ex to have her stuff. I was selling all of it. It was a nice burden to lift from my shoulders, and it was going to be great having my garage available to me. One newcomer came over and held up a pair of shoes and asked the same, "How much?" as the last lady. "Oh, fifty cents." She was shocked. "Sir, this Coach! It espensive!" Wow, these people were so honest they knew they were making out like bandits. I responded the same way I did before, telling her it's a dollar. She reacted the same. I sold all the purses, shoes, and most of the soaps and lotions and made around 75 bucks at the end of the day. That should tell you the number of things on hand versus selling for a buck or less. I felt accomplished today.

My divorce hearing was to be finalized on Halloween Day. October 31st was always one of my favorite holidays, and it just got that much sweeter. Me and my girlfriend attended a convention together, which was horror themed. I got to meet one of my heroes from the Ghostbusters, Ernie Hudson, as well as the great Doug Jones. I also met Margot Kidder, among other stars. I used the money from my garage sale to pay for meet and greets, signed photos, and more. I went crazy because it was feel good money. I made my costume this time. My new girlfriend was going to be attending this one with me and suggested Mortal Kombat, so I threw down Sub Zero. The fact she suggested my favorite fighting game was also a solid sign this was a good relationship. She went as Mileena, and even Drew showed up as Jax. This was their first convention and only my second. We had a blast, took a ton of great photos, and met some new awesome friends. I even joined a Ghostbuster Group who I met at the event, but that is its own story for a different book.

Halloween day came up quick. The decorations were out, the candy was purchased, and I was ready. I wasn't ready for trick or treating, I was ready for court. I dressed in my cleanest Army uniform I owned, went to court, and prepared for the craziest day of my life. My attorney met up with me, and we went to the courtroom. It was empty, no witnesses, no jury, just the two of us. I'm not sure what I was expecting, I guess all of my other experiences in court were full of people, even traffic court since I liked to Ricky Bobby my way down the highway.

The judge arrived, we did the formalities, rising for the judge, seating, and so forth. My ex was nowhere to be seen. Was she not coming? Was I a free man? The judge looked up and asked if all parties were present and we said here. There was no other acknowledgment. He continued and read the divorce decree. He read the terms of the divorce out loud and asked if there was any question to what was being written. I said there were no concerns from my end. The other side of the room was silent, considering it was empty. He finished the terms and rounded to the end of the process. "Does anyone in this courtroom object to the findings by this court, or contest to any of the terms detailed in the decree previously gone over in detail?" He looked at me, and said "Mister Carpenter, do you have any objections or additional information at this time?" I said no. He looked over at the empty desk. "Mrs. Carpenter are there any objections or additional information you would like to supply at this time?" The empty desk did not answer. Wow, this judge had a sense of humor and already knew exactly how this was playing out, given the backstory he knew from my opening statement. He awarded me the divorce, decreed on Halloween Day. The day of freedom.

I honestly thought this was over, my struggle, my pain, it ended on Halloween. Being we were legally separated for good, the Big D, she should have disappeared, and I would carry on with my life. She didn't take divorce too lightly apparently and contested it for the next few weeks with the lawyer. I paid my last payment to the office, and they told me that she had an unfair trial and wants a retrial. They also let her know that it doesn't work that way. All she had to do was show up. She said the big lawyer words confused her and it wasn't fair. I laughed and even mentioned that they told her to seek legal counsel over the phone, in front of me. I was already happy with the Bank Girl, whom I was still seeing, and things were going very well.

In November, I made a decision. I have no idea why or what compelled me to not wait. I asked the Banker Girl to marry me. I was going to make Audrey, the Banker Girl, my wife. She had a hell of a personality, was a go-getter, had a steady job, and best of all, I loved who I was when I was with her. I can't say the same for my ex. We had dated for 7 years before I married her and regretted every single day. I was told to not rush things and date for a while until I knew who this new girl really was. I provided my friends and family with my previous numbers. Dating for four months is a roll of the dice, but I had a good feeling about this one.

Shortly after going public on Facebook that we were dating, I proposed. Of course, long-distance friends who weren't in the loop thought I proposed within five minutes of dating. Honestly, five minutes is what it felt like given the four months' worth of time we shared together. Things were going great, I spent Thanksgiving with her and her family, and they were all amazing. I got along with everyone. It's a shame they were Cowboys fans though. Either way, they were all great. Her cousins were pretty cool and were almost like older brothers since she was an only child. We moved onward and spent Christmas together. This was an entire 180 from the previous Christmas. I even got a custom Baltimore Ravens jersey from my fiancée. Ages ago for Christmas, I would provide a list of what I was into. My ex would be stupid and buy every single thing on the list. I gave a small list of things to Audrey that I thought were cool and got one or two of these things, one being the jersey. She was already smarter, which wasn't hard to do.

In the new year, I got a call from my ex. She still floated around and apparently made it a point to know she existed. I picked up the phone. The last time we talked, I was yelled at about the divorce, so I can't imagine what this was about. She cut right to the point. "I don't know anyone else to call. I can't really tell my family how I really feel. I just miss being able to talk to you." I told her that ship sailed ages ago, but I'll listen since she has me. "Well, Latin Lover hit me. He beat me, and I don't know what to do." I smiled. This was my moment. "Well, now you know what it really feels like. I never hit you. This is coming back around after all of those reports." She got quiet, and maybe I shouldn't have taken the petty low blow. I asked, "Are you ok?" She said not really because it's out of control and her family even saw it. Ooh, witnesses, I like where this is going. I continued to talk to her for more info.

It turns out, Noni was in the hospital. This was the first I was hearing about it, but I also wasn't privy to much information given the circumstances. She fell and fell hard. She didn't get back up from this. I got serious. I sat down to talk because I needed to know more about this. Screw her getting smacked around by Latin Lover. She said she didn't think Noni was coming out of the hospital, so she had been spending as much time with her as possible, which was understandable. One particular day she went from work, which she apparently worked at a deli in Pennsylvania where her family moved, to the hospital. Latin Lover was not a happy camper about not having dinner ready for him and stormed to the hospital. He smacked her around in front of the whole family waiting in the waiting room. I assumed this was true because why would you call me and tell me as your ex-husband?

Noni wasn't in a good place mentally the last few days apparently. She was losing more of her mental faculties as the days waned on. While Noni was in the hospital, my ex was visiting with Latin Lover, and she asked who he was. She said who he was, which was a friend, and Noni asked "Well, where is Harry? Can he come in?" See, me and this woman had a bond. I was the only one to listen to her long old lady stories. I found her interesting. She was from the motherland of Italy and had lived a very long life of adventure. She learned English and spoke fluent Italian. She was one of the good ones. She told her Noni that I had died in combat, and she instantly lost it. She had to correct herself and say she was kidding and that we were no longer together, which still upset her. To know that woman was potentially on her deathbed asking for me was heartbreaking. I couldn't go visit, not without risking my life being around her family. I even felt the need to apologize for how I hung up our big blow up call in the summer, since I felt so bad. Ok, back to the reason she actually called.

Her boy toy, whom she potentially married from stories I heard, got upset about the lack of dinner, smacked her around, and here we were. She wanted advice, or help, or something, but I could offer her nothing. What could I do, other than offer a big 'I told you so" from my position? I'm not sure how things played out with the dude. After a while, they were no longer together. I heard word she had him sent back to his homeland and heard other stories that she had him deported. As far as I was concerned, they weren't together anymore. Sure enough, she asked if we were able to try to work things out and try again. I knew it. It was hiding in the sad story. The remorse, the rehashing of good times we had, all of it. It all reeked of ulterior motive. I told her no. I was actually with someone now. She got infuriated and said, "I hope that little slut is happy with you," and hung up the phone. Well, there is the ex I know. She was hiding under the tears and sadness waiting to spring out.

We decided to marry at the end of April, which wasn't that far away. It gave us about five months to plan the wedding, and I was going to take the reins. This one was going to go smoother because I had been through the wringer the first time trying to plan the last one years ago. I knew the steps and what to do at this point. Me and Audrey were looking all over the United States at nice places to do this thing. We looked in Maryland, Florida, and New Mexico. We even toyed around with the idea of a Vegas Wedding. We got real and tried to hone in on something local since her family was much bigger than mine. It made no sense to fly that many people across the world. We settled on New Mexico and looked at Santa Fe. We were pretty dead set on this scenic place with waterfalls, a nice lake, mountains in the distance, and more.

We had a change in my unit. The first sergeant and Commander were both replaced by two new guys, both super hardcore former Infantry or Ranger guys. The new first sergeant and this captain both came from a hardcore breed and were a change of pace from the last two, the pro wrestler and good ol' boy, whom I liked. It didn't really seem to faze me, and not much really changed with our unit and the goings on, which was a relief. In addition to this, my ex vanished, it seemed, after the last phone call at the start of the year. It was now almost March, and we were coming around to my birthday once again. Me and Audrey spent Valentine's Day together, and had a great time, unlike last year being told about having a better time with the boyfriend. The year was coming together nicely, filling with better holiday memories than the previous. Then it happened; we were going off to Fort Stewart, Georgia to do a month-long training exercise. I had a damn wedding to plan.

CHAPTER 17

Let's Try This Again, With Feeling

I flew out as the advanced party for setting up of the whole training operation. I went out almost a week sooner than the rest of the unit and that cut into my time even harder. Luckily, we had already decided on a venue in Las Cruces, a nice little historic Victorian house. We even had ideas on a caterer, so the hard parts were sorted out. I was still pissed about having to go to Georgia but went anyhow because what are you gonna do? I landed in what I am going to describe as a damn swamp. I was waiting for Shrek to greet us at any moment and tell us to get out of his home. There were gnats, mosquitoes, and wet hot heat. It was muggy the whole time out there. The ground was always squishy and swampy, but we made the best of it.

I had my first Yuengling beer in a long time while out there since they don't carry it in El Paso. I made the best of it, and eventually, the unit showed up for work. We were setting up on what turned out to be a marshland swampy area, but no one was the wiser. We set up the tents, computers, and any other equipment we needed. Our section was off to the back. We had our own tent away from the rest of the unit, as they weren't on a need to know basis; they just needed to have the end result. I worked nights, as it was what I knew, and Sergeant Slaughter took the day shift and worked with a supporting soldier from the unit. I still didn't have enough rank to be anything import-ant, but I had the ability to run a shift as I did in Iraq. On a few occasions, the new commander came in, made small talk and joked with us. I really didn't have an issue with this guy, he seemed pretty ok. We survived the field exercise. I even saw a gator for the first time in the wild. We flew back after celebrat-ing my birthday in the swamp. My fiancée had a belated birth-day meal set up for me when I got back, which was nice. We were a month away from the wedding at this point.

Having only a month left meant we needed to buckle down and set things up. Her mom hooked us up with a DJ, and her dad won us a contest on the radio station for a wedding con-vention. I had never been to one of these, but we went in ready for anything. We found the idea for a photo booth and got a caterer locked in. Our entry apparently gave us a chance at a contest later in the event. With the radio win, we got two en-tries. They began calling the names, and we were picked as one of the couples. We did trivia, which we totally crushed. Having such a huge point lead, we went into the coupon clipping round and completed first and dominated. I will boast for yet another time: we crushed those other couples. We beat them so bad, they doubted everything in life and probably hated coupons for the rest of their existence. Ok, I'm done now.

Part of our victory prize was an all-expenses-paid trip to Niagara Falls. The other part was a bunch of gift certificates to a cake maker and a party supply store. We were beyond grate-ful, even to this day, because that seriously cut out the expenses we had for the wedding. The radio even invited us on the air to speak about being the big winners, and that was pretty cool too. We were in wedding mode at this point. I had family and friends flying in throughout the week leading up to the event. I requested off for that Wednesday prior up through the Monday after, which I thought wasn't too bad to be missing from work for four days trying to coordinate a wedding. Another fun fact:

I was around six months shy of getting out of the Army, which meant I could begin out-processing and get my foot out of the door, in a manner of speaking. I was going to handle that piece after the wedding in May after the honeymoon, and other things were over.

I wasn't home more than a week when the command staff announced another field exercise. You can see why I still hate camping to this day. I had been on one in November, January, February, March, and now another one in April? I'm being trained to death. The dates were going to be from the second week of April to the end of the First week of May, literally over top of the wedding. I had my leave denied and the wedding vacation was off. I hit panic mode, and this was when I started to not like being in the Army more than ever before. Support my ex-wife? Shame on you. Shit upon my new one and screw my wedding plans up? Not on my watch.

I had to be smart about this. I knew I wasn't getting exempt from the entire field exercise. Since we had a new Platoon Sergeant as well, I couldn't pull favors. I spoke to the new PS, and we agreed to have me go out to the field to run the night operations, as I always did under one condition; I can leave that Wednesday as originally agreed upon. I was to report to work formation in the morning and head out afterward to get my wedding duties done. That seemed like a fair deal. The only things that changed for me were going to the field and reporting back on Thursday and Friday. I could do that, and I would also try to out processes medically while I'm in the neighborhood, since I have to come back into work anyway.

The days went by, and I worked a lot in the field. I was up for a few days at a time to ensure I worked both day and night shift. Slaughter was off training on the new equipment across the base with our other guy. No biggie, as I filled in for him quite well. Slaughter eventually joined us for a day or two just to see how things were rolling. I told him about the plans the platoon sergeant and I made, and he acknowledged the only way he knew how: "Word." We were set, as it was finally the week of the wedding day, and now presently it was that Wednesday during the day. I packed my belongings and brought them to work with me, ready to check out with the last shuttle bus back to base. I approached the sergeant and told him a report of what we were doing, any further data he needed, and that everything is in order. Slaughter was due to return to pick up for the final week, so everything should be going great. We agreed, and he helped me board the bus at around 11 pm, bound for the base.

I got home super late, went to bed, and woke up once again at the crack of dawn. I got dressed in uniform, headed to the formation, gave my accountability per our agreement, and checked out. The first day, Thursday, I hit the medical staff and was medically cleared for pending discharge. This meant I could no longer go to the field, do physical fitness, or anything that could put me in harm's way because this was a big no-no for the Army to hurt me after getting an evaluation of my current health. I made my way to the airport to pick up K, who I invited to be a groomsman/woman. Still no word from Miguel, who was my Best Man, since he didn't get the chance to be at the first wedding. My dad flew in on Friday and stayed at a hotel at the edge of town with his wife and my half-brother. It took me years to get over that whole ordeal, but I'm glad they were all able to make it. My mom refused to fly out, and my grandparents were not in the best of health to hit the road to New Mexico.

Friday, we all went out to a Mexican restaurant called La Posta. Everyone had a blast, we did the rehearsal things, and we all knew what to do. We decorated the venue as best as possible the night before. Thankfully we got chair covers with our rental company certificate, otherwise, the place would have looked like butt. The house was a very awesome place. The owner or caretaker had the greatest stories and was apparently a vocal coach for famous singers. He had stories for days and gave us the tour of the house as he told them. We were ready for the next day. Still no word from Miguel.

We had arranged for my future wife and I to have a room at the house as well as her parents for the night of the wedding, so we could party all night and pass out on site. Miguel had booked a room for the night before and night of, however. The only concern was K, who was going to fly out late that night. Thankfully, my dad stepped in and offered her a lift to the airport once the festivities were at a close. We had everything under control, apart from one person. The venue was beautiful at night with all of the lights inside and out, and we knew it would look awesome the next day. After the dinner, we retired back to our respective locations; me at my house with K on the couch, my lady with her parents at her house, and my dad at their hotel. It wasn't until late in the night, I found out the only trouble I had.

Miguel apparently flew in. This was only after missing his initial flight, and several additional flights to follow. He was more or less influenced to join me at the behest of his current girlfriend, who also flew with him. They arrived at the bed and breakfast that we were using for the wedding and beat on the door in the twilight of the night. The owner opened the door and apparently, words were exchanged, but he was able to stay the night. The next day, Miguel got up late. He took forever to get ready but managed to help me decorate the final touches of the reception area, as well as the altar. We had an officiant scheduled for the wedding time. The DJ was set up outside at the altar on the steps as well as inside the reception hall. Catering was loading in and family and friends were arriving. This was going so smooth. The owner of the venue even offered a fancy sports car to drop off my bride to be at the front gate to walk down the aisle with her dad. This was magical.

During the beginning before she was ready to walk down

the aisle, I had to keep hunting down her mom who wandered off every five seconds. Short of that, I had no issues. They started playing the music she requested to walk down the aisle to, and I jumped back in place. She came through the gates, and she was beautiful. She and her dad walked down the aisle, and he wore his sunglasses. While Joe Cool was walking her down the aisle, Miguel leaned forward and said, "Dude, Audrey is hot man. Congrats." This was the first time he had ever seen her, so it was more of a surprise for him than me. I leaned back and whispered, "I know," and the ceremony was to start.

Audrey was released by her dad. She started up the two steps to the altar, of course, tripping up the stairs. She was clumsy, so I came to discover early on. On one occasion, she lost her balance in my hallway and ping-ponged off each wall on the way to the bathroom, so I figured she would at least trip up the stairs. We started the ceremony, and the officiant read off the words we had chosen together. Audrey was crying, and I motioned for her family to pass some tissue up through the bridesmaids. Her nose kept running and we even motioned to pause things for a moment, but this lady kept on going with the ceremony. After the runny nose was plugged, we tuned back into the rest of the ordeal, just in time to get to the presentation of the rings.

She received my ring from her Maid of Honor, one of her high school and college friends. I didn't know them too much, but her people seemed like good people. I reached back to ask Miguel for the ring, and he plopped the ring box into my hand. Like, literally, still in the cardboard box that protected that velvet box, into my hand. You can even hear me on the wedding video say, "Fuck is wrong with you, take it out the damn box." He quickly fixed it, handed me the ring, and we completed the ceremony. Everything went so well. We went to the reception and were introduced as Husband and Wife to Avenged Sevenfold, and I knew this was going to be an awesome life from here on out. It turns out, my wedding was the first one Miguel had ever been to, let alone been a major player in. Good thing we got that out of the way before his brother got married years later, otherwise, that would have been awkward.

The reception went very well, and my father-in-law and I even had a dance-off at one point. Everyone was happy. We now have hundreds of photo booth photos, wedding photographer photos, and great video. I invited mainly Army buddies, like Drew and his wife, Sergeant Slaughter and family, and Rob and his soon to be wife just a short few weeks later. We even invited the radio DJ's because, without that contest, we wouldn't have all of this awesomeness available. At some point in the night I was even approached by two people, who I assumed were with my wife, and they introduced themselves as the Wedding Crashers. They said they were having a blast, and that this was the best wedding they ever crashed. Heck, these two even signed the guestbook and took photos in the photo booth. What a hell of a night!

The next morning we went out for pancakes. Everyone was fairly hung over. The owner of the home said I must have had at least 23 beers that he could count, as he was watching from the balcony of the top floor looking over the whole event. He also half expected me and her dad to fight, as is the tradition to have a fight at a wedding, but nothing happened. I realized how drunk I had been because we couldn't even figure out the air conditioner the night before. These were much-needed pancakes.

The weekend had passed, and I was still on euphoria from the whole ordeal. I had an awesome wife, and I had an awesome time with everyone that came out. Now, as it was Monday, it was time to go back to work. I reported in, per our agreement, because I hadn't forgotten. Somehow today, today was different. I was called out of ranks, told to report to first sergeant's office after formation was over, and I did. I went to meet him in his office, and there was my Platoon Sergeant in there as well. "Why did you go off and get married? I explicitly told you not to. Did you disobey an order?" the first sergeant said. "No, I worked it out with my chain of command and only missed out on two days. I am willing to return to the field if necessary, but I already medically cleared." His vein in his forehead grew four sizes at that moment.

My platoon sergeant spoke up. "I never gave him permission to do anything like that, he's lying." Other staff in the admin room were also stunned. They were pretty sure that conversation happened because it seemed fair. They also believed it to be a fair trade since I could have medically cleared before going to the field training. Instead, I chose to work my butt off for three weeks with them. My jaw dropped after hearing those words come from his face. I was told I'd be facing a demotion, what they call an Article 15, and I was in deep doo-doo. I left out of the office in a huff. I wasn't having any more of this crap. On my way out, the re-enlistment representative happened to catch me, because I was still within that window as well. I told them to stick it, as I went to my car and drove off. I eventually did apologize to her and told her what happened a month or two later. It was too late to consider signing back up at that time.

Apparently, Rob told the big boss man that he had several years left on his contract and was going to Afghanistan with the rest of the gang in October. It was known that the two of us were in for the same time, signed up at the same time, and were practically the same down the line. We both were going to be getting out at the same time unless he re-enlisted, which he didn't. This was the reason that first sergeant was pissed, and I figured it best to show him my military papers to absolve myself. I printed out my Records Briefing, which showed practically everything about me including my end of contract date, dated a few months from now. They had already shortened contracts by three months. So instead of February, I was now set to be out by November, pushing up my timeline a bit.

He was not happy and said I falsified that document and doesn't believe it. He made my life a living hell for the next three months. I was persecuted, harassed, punished, and tormented for much of the rest of my army time. This was a huge issue with my post-wedding plans, since I tried to go to Niagara Falls, and that was a hard battle. Luckily, I was able to get the commander and a few other Sergeants to sign off on it, and I went to Niagara. I wasn't thrilled to know I was coming back to that disaster in combat boots, however.

I received a letter in the mail from the Army Tricare healthcare office, stating what my expenses would be if I wasn't covered by their crappy insurance. I don't know why they send these passive aggressive letters, but this was actually useful. On it was a list of medications such as blood pressure medication, diabetes testing strips, insulin, Valtrex, and an antidepressant. They were under my ex's name, which I figured the dead giveaway was the beetus testing supplies. These prescriptions racked up a total of over 1800 bucks a month if we hadn't had Tricare coverage. The drugs were being filled at some CVS in Pennsylvania, so there was no doubt about it. I had to put a huge stop on this little gravy trains tracks.

I made my way to update my dependent information with the Army. Not only did I need to add my current wife, but I also needed to find out how the hell my Ex was still receiving benefits. The representative said I still had my ex listed, and whoever did it apparently didn't fully delete her off my records. She was living with Army benefits for the past few months with nothing in her way. I was livid. How the hell does this even happen? I specifically came in here to do that way back last year in November before going to the field for training. There is one thing I can assure you about the Army: they will lose your paperwork at least ten times. Keep a backup. I turned in another divorce decree as well as a marriage license, which I'm sure looked great at the time.

As it turns out, they were able to retroactively cancel everything. It officially said on record that she lacked coverage since October 31, 2011, and that was music to my ears. I got everything updated, got in my car, and called that pharmacy. The lady on the phone was super nice. I gave her the claim number and my identifying information for Tricare. She pulled up my Ex and all of her info since I was the primary provider on the account they could have no trouble accessing it. I told the pharmacy assistant she was not covered and has not been since October. "Oh, my oh my." She said. "She was just in here with you yesterday to pick up her medications, why didn't you say anything then?" I couldn't believe it. I had to update this poor woman on this fraud going on. "Well, that wasn't me. Can you describe the guy who was me for me?" She said "A short stocky Spanish fellow. He had a few piercings and a lot of tattoos, and I didn't know you could have those in the Army. My nephew is in the Coast Guard, and they are very strict on those kinds of things, but I wasn't sure what the rules were." This dude was running around posing as me for the last time. He signed off on a new car as me. He is getting prescriptions as me. I thought my ex had him removed? Apparently, they were still together, even after the smacking around incident. Was it all made up? Thankfully she was able to update the records, and I faxed her over proof later that afternoon. She told me the pharmacist would be in touch with all of her care providers and update their records. She had a lot of doctors considering they were free.

A few weeks after going to Niagara and dealing with this benefits fiasco, Audrey was staying over at my house. She still worked at the same bank in New Mexico. It was much harder for me to stay over during the week, being in the Army and whatnot. They could call me back at the drop of a hat if need be. I would, however, stay over on some weekends. This would leave her to stay the night on a few weeknights. We made this work as best as possible, given the distance. She didn't want to leave her job, and I couldn't leave mine. It was only for a few months; what harm was it going to do?

Audrey left at the crack of dawn, as she always did, to make it back to her side of town to work. I woke up around the same time for morning formation, which was the fitness first call of the day. I did the thing and had to work as a road guard for the PT time to ensure I stopped traffic and all of that. They found a need for me, even if I technically couldn't run or work out with them. After the all-clear was given, I headed home to eat breakfast and watch some TV before our 9 AM work call. There was a knock on the door, and on the other side, I was greeted by two Military Police Officers. "Specialist how are you this morning. Is your wife home?" They were able to identify me by the uniform, but I answered them back "No, she left for work hours ago." They stood straight up and stopped leaning on the outside door frame. "May we come into your home?"

I allowed them to come in, but I asked them what this was all about. "Well, we got a call earlier from Mrs. Carpenter. Is she home?" I reiterated she was not and had already left for work. They started walking through the house, checking different rooms as they told me why they were there. "She reported that you struck her this morning. Is this true?" I was pissed. I was not doing this again. This girl is messing with the wrong person because I just got rid of my ex, and I'm not standing for these shenanigans from another woman. I asked them when this happened because I needed times. "It happened around 0600 this morning. You said she is at work?" As they were looking around, I still had a ton of wedding stuff left out like photos, programs, and gifts. "So, your wife's name is Audrey?" I acknowledged that it was. "Hmm. Interesting." I asked the Sergeant officer "The name on the report isn't Audrey is it?" He looked at me and said,

"I can't confirm or deny that information buddy," as he shook his head no. I told him that my ex-wife was constantly calling the police on me and harassing me for a very long time. I asked if it was her name on that report from this morning. "Unfortunately, I cannot disclose that information. If I were you, I'd do my best to protect myself legally from these reports happening any further." As he said this he nodded his head yes. I knew it.

She was still harassing me. Why wouldn't she go away? I figured what it was is that every time I got something cleaned up, and it affected her in some way, she would retaliate. Each time she would milk the system and it backfired, she would retaliate. I was so glad it wasn't Audrey because I was not about to do this again. I told her all about it that night, and she was worried about what my ex might do in the future. What steps would she take to be malicious? These were legitimate concerns of Audrey's and also mine now that they were brought up.

Even after I was remarried, I still had to go to my classes per the Army. I went to several counseling courses that were mandated, but I didn't mind them anymore. It was more people watching than being angry about being there, plus it got me out of work for a while. We would play with Play-Doh and mold our emotions. I would always make a Play-Doh poop because it was how I felt about things. I was also not good at molding with that stuff either. My skills were limited. I figured I was done with my ex after that ordeal because nothing from my end should be affecting her at this point, but I was wrong.

She called me one night to tell me Noni had passed away in the hospital. She held on for several months but ultimately didn't make it. I was heartbroken. I would have loved to see that woman, whether she was family or not. I even wanted to fly up and visit her and pay my respects at her funeral, but in the interest of my safety, I opted out. My ex kept the call short and sweet and limited it to just that blurb of news. I thanked her for letting me know. We ended the call, very somber and civil. It was probably the only time she was tolerable. I even told Audrey about it, not trying to give the impression I was attached to my ex, but rather, just the family member who I cherished for 11 years. My emotions were all over the place. It was a rough time.

CHAPTER 18

Home Again, Home Again, Jiggity Jig

I started to round out the tail end of my Army career. I put up with first sergeants bullshit for far too long, and he was starting to get on everyone else's nerves, too. He said something in formation to the effect of "I will crucify you like Jesus to the cross." Apparently, that was the breaking point for someone as they reported it to the high command staff. In this letter, they talked about all the offensive things he's done, said, and even how he persecuted me for absolutely no reason. Just like that, he was removed from command in the middle of August. One of the other sergeants got to step up. Let me say, had he been in charge all this time, I'd have signed back up and gone to Afghanistan for that man. He had my respect.

I received a court summons due to my ex not appearing for any of the classes or community service. She had broken her end of the deal for the assault case. Quite frankly, I had forgotten all about that drama. I took an entire workday off and went to court. I hopped in the elevator and went to the appropriate floor. There she was. Sitting across the hallway from me, with her stupid lawyer. Her attorney saw me and walked over. "So, how are you doing?" I gave her one-word answers. I said I was good. "Great, glad to hear. So, I heard the two of you recently divorced. Is that true?" I said "Yes. And it's been damn near a year, and a good one at that." I felt like I was being interrogated. I stuck with short answers. "Oh, you have a wedding band on, did you remarry?" I just said yes and started playing on my phone. This lady needed to scram. She eventually took the hint and went back to my ex and started talking to her.

They called my ex to go into the courtroom. Now, let me set the visual for what she decided to wear to the court that day. She wore a skin-tight purple dress that cut off at the upper thigh, with her assets hanging out of the top. She wore a gaudy gold belt around her waist, from Claire's or something, and furry high heeled boots. This was a court hearing, not the corner where you were turning tricks. The greatest moment, however, came when she got up to go across the room. My Ex dropped her handful of papers. She bent down to pick them up, and that little cheap Claire's belt exploded off her body like a damn grenade full of bits of shrapnel. I think the dress may have also split.

They went in and I was never called. I eventually went to the lady at the podium and asked what the deal was. They took me back to the state's attorney and we discussed some things. Apparently, her attorney motioned for an extension because clearly, she was dressed like a hooker. I wasn't sure that was the exact reason, but they asked to postpone this ordeal for a week. I ended up bringing Audrey to the next trip because she wanted to see this girl. They were a no show. Apparently, they requested another extension to drag the case out further. I never did get to see this play out in court.

The last few weeks of my time I spent getting things in order such as moving, clearing the checklist like housing, military gear issue, and more. Our interim first sergeant came into the office frequently and would ask "Carpenter, what the hell are you doing here. Don't you have an appointment? Out of my sight." I didn't even have an appointment, but I got the pleasure of enjoying my last few weeks as a soldier sitting around and watching TV and playing video games. Life was going well again, but I wasn't going to be much longer in this military world to see it. I used my leave and was able to check out the first week or two of September. I received my discharge paperwork, effective fully at the end of November. I didn't have to go back to work anymore. I worked to pack up my house using one of those PODS and moved in with my wife and her family before heading to Maryland.

We drove in separate cars back to Maryland, me with my guitar and TV, her with her cat, Chubs. Chubs was a cool cat. Her real name was Destiny, but because she was fat her nickname was Chubs, or rather, The Chubs to be exact. Once we hit the road, the cat chewed out of the carrier. She did not want to be in that thing. We stopped off at Walmart and grabbed a heavy-duty plastic one, as opposed to the cushy fabric one we chose in the beginning. We were halfway back through El Paso when I got a phone call again from my wife. "The cat just shit. It smells horrible please help me." We pulled into a gas station. Sure enough, that cat was covered in an entire gut full of fecal matter. There was poop everywhere. It was so bad; the cat didn't want to clean herself. I put her in the sink, and she went with it. We cleaned the cat, hit the road, and I swear she didn't take a dump the entire rest of the way back.

We made it to Maryland and were set up to stay with my grandparents for a bit until we got an apartment. This worked out since Audrey already got an interview with a bank and landed the job instantly. One of us had a job, the other had a paycheck for another two months. We could do this. We pulled up to my Grandparents' house and loaded our few belongings in. I built a replica Ghostbusters Proton Pack and loaded that into the house, too. I had a TV, Guitar, and movie props. These were clearly the necessities of life. We were holed up in the small spare back room at my grandparents' house. You could hear everything. Everything we did was loud. If we rolled over, if we whispered, anything, it was loud. Apparently, our cat was a menace to her cat. We needed to get out of this place and fast.

We were in that house no more than a few days before we landed an apartment just down the street. They were really nice, quiet, and the floor plan was solid. Our POD showed up after a huge headache a few days before Christmas. I went to work unloading it and putting furniture in. We eventually went out and found a nice solid table at Goodwill, which we still have to this day for 20 bucks. We purchased a bedroom set, and it really was feeling like a done deal with being adults. This is what marriage must feel like, or what it's supposed to feel like.

Even in Maryland, my wife lived for concerts. She purchased tickets to go up to a place called Steel Stacks, or something to that effect to see Avenged Sevenfold and a few other bands. See, that was her band, and she would follow them to the ends of the earth to watch them perform. They weren't bad, but not my favorite. Audrey drove us up there, we spent the night, went to the concert the following day, and drove back. I was having a blast with her and the new life we were making in Maryland. This would seem like the last bit of the story also, but it's not. Please stick with me for this one. We stopped into Office Depot. I used to work there back in the day and might know people, and because I needed school supplies for the school I was planning to attend. I didn't know what I would actually need, so I planned to grab the basics. They also had camera memory cards on sale for dirt cheap. Since Audrey took ten billion photos, she was about due for a new card. We pulled into the Bel Air Office Depot on the way home.

We walked into the store, and it happened. It was my Spider-Sense. It was that feeling Ron Swanson got when Tammy 2 was in the building. I knew something was amiss. I looked out of the corner of my eye, and there she was. My Ex. I told Audrey "That's her," because the two of them never formally met or had seen each other in person. My ex took off running, she bowled through a few people and disappeared to the back of the store. I shrugged my shoulders and just went shopping with my wife, undeterred by the chance encounter. I was surrounded by a few employees who constantly asked if I needed help with anything. I invented this tactic, gentlemen, it's called a Code 5, and no, I'm not stealing anything. Code 5 was my and a few co-workers made up name for a theft, otherwise known as a 5-finger discount. I invented this thing, back off me.

We picked up the purchases, headed to the car, loaded up Audrey's Mazda, and went to go look at kitties at the PetSmart next door. We finished there and headed home. That was a hell of an encounter. The drive home consisted of Audrey asking about her and me wondering how the hell she even got a job back at Office Depot. None of that mattered. We drove across the Inner Harbor and back to our quiet little apartment.

I was now a full-time student at the community college living off the GI Bill, and Audrey was working at a bank in Baltimore. We were in a decent place financially and things were going well, all things considered. Eventually, she got tired of seeing me sitting on my butt and playing video games, so I interviewed for a job working as a Third-Party Retailer. One particular day returning from class, I grabbed the mail on the way in. In that stack of papers, was a giant brown envelope. It was addressed from the Circuit Courts of York County, PA to me. I opened it up, and I could not believe what I was looking at. It was a court summons to appear in court for a domestic violence charge. The date of the court date? Today, at 1 PM. It was 5 by the time I checked the mail.

I started drinking heavily. I must have had six or seven Yuengling's before Audrey got home from the bank. The papers said if I failed to show up to court, there would be a warrant for my arrest. It also read that I should be considered armed and dangerous. She was visibly shaken by the whole ordeal and told me to keep my head on straight, I've defeated her before. She was like a comic book villain, always popping up at the most inconvenient times, but she was right. I could get through this, too. I pulled out a notepad and began reading through the charges and claims. I looked for inconsistencies and boy were there plenty. I got writing as quick as I could.

For starters, it was addressed to Private Carpenter, US Army, Texas. No wonder I never got the damn thing. Do you know how many of us there are, and how many military bases are in Texas, the biggest damn state in the union? Second, It's Specialist. I was promoted while we were married when I was in Iraq, but obviously, you didn't care to notice. I took note of the postmarked date too. It was sent out two days ago, not enough time to even prepare for a court case, take off work, or whatever would need to be done. I hadn't even gotten into the meat of the document, this was just the envelope.

I dissected the whole thing from start to finish. The first thing I noticed, my birthday is wrong. Eleven years together and you don't know my damn birthday? Not enough to dismiss this case in court, but something of note to correct. She had my correct social security number, which was correct only due to maybe being on some tax form or something she had. We got into the juicy stuff, where she details what happened and what went down. I read the whole thing easily four times. As I started to sober up a bit, things were clear enough to see what was wrong.

She gave her statement to the effect of "I came into the store and rushed towards her aggressively. I grabbed her and threw her through a display, and she screamed for help. A few customers and employees grabbed me and dragged me away, but I overpowered them with my Army training and ran after her again. I chased her to the women's room where I didn't follow, and she was able to call the police. I ran out of the emergency exit once I heard cop sirens and hopped into my Chevy Cavalier and sped off back to Texas." That was a lot to unpack right there.

For starters, I was with my wife, which was excluded entirely. She ran off and hid in the women's room and I stopped chasing her then? A door with a ladies room sticker on it would stop a madman like me on a rampage? There was so much to pick apart. The biggest one is that she saw my car, which I sold and have since upgraded. I also could speak to the part where she said I had a house full of guns because I didn't have one. It was a good thing my wife told me to pick this thing apart, and I planned to call the Sheriff the very next day.

I called the office of the Sheriff and spoke to him directly. I explained that I just received the letter yesterday evening, and I wasn't allowed the time to even speak my case. He said that it's a common tactic from prosecuting attorneys that represent women in PA since they have a battered women's law and a few other protective things in place. I updated my address and personal information with him and told him what really went down. He even said that it makes more sense that I live in Maryland, rather than the scenario she described. Honestly, her way made me sound very nutso. He said he would investigate it, not to worry, and he will give me a call in a few days.

I waited around for a few days and sure enough, he called. I still hadn't gotten a call from that retail job yet and even asked if this was something that would appear on a background check. He said the system doesn't work that fast, even on a good day. The good news was, he filed to contest the court findings due to lack of evidence. He explained to me that he put in a few calls to the Harford County PD, and they have no record of the phone call or dispatch to that location. He also had them check the store, where no employee came forward with any statement to support. They don't even remember me at all, or the rampage through the aisles. Lastly, on his end, she waited almost two whole weeks to report this incident. Checkmate. We had a hearing set for a few weeks from now. I finally got hired on for good at my job and started working right away, a week before Black Friday.

I was a "Store Manager" and even had hiring rights. I brought on a classmate and one of my friends, Frank. These two guys were phenomenal salesmen. We were killing it and making a ton of money in commissions and bonuses, and I was still receiving money for going to school. I went off to PA for the court case and won, on the grounds of she was an idiot. They picked her whole story apart and realized that it was a false report. I didn't even need a lawyer, and I thank that Sheriff for doing his due diligence. Pennsylvania doesn't allow a false reporting crime because of the type of reporting it was. They don't want to discourage women from reporting abusive men. I was screwed on that option, but I understood it.

A few weeks later at work, I met this lady, Renee, who was one of my employees and a real estate agent. I mentioned in passing that eventually, we were looking at houses. She started to compile some ideas, nothing serious, but just idea gathering about what the ideal home would be. I needed a decent neighborhood, a garage or some sort of area to store nerdy things that I was collecting, and a deck for the parties I planned to throw.

My birthday came and went. I had a Superhero Bowling party, which was unique, and everyone had a blast. I was truly blessed and had some amazing friends. We went to friends' houses for the Fourth of July and celebrated friendship and Murika. Unfortunately, I did have to stop going to class since working retail didn't jive well with a set school schedule. I postponed my education and focused on running this store thing. We did so well, I even got to be the regional trainer for the area in September and October. We even purchased that house in August!

Things were going very well for us, best they had ever been. Then the news hit. In mid-October, it was announced to the managers that this partnership with the major retail store was to be no more, and we were officially to be done the week before Black Friday. I was also told not to tell my staff. I immediately told everyone because I believed they also needed time to find a job, much as I did. It was a devastating blow for all of us.

Luckily, I had a few prospective jobs lined up pretty quickly. I had a third-party retailer job inside a Best Buy selling Apple Products and Staples. Given my experience with office supplies and technology, I shouldn't have an issue with either of them. I interviewed, and both wanted me. What a time to be alive, to be wanted by two jobs. I shifted towards the job that was giving me a better job title. Staples would be bringing me on as Assistant Store Manager. I interviewed, and the people loved me. I was told they needed to run a background check and a few other things, and they would announce a hiring date. I was happy to hold a job before I even lost my current one because life doesn't work like that. So, it seems my life is perfect and working out great and this is the end of the book, but that would not be an accurate statement. I was delighted to head home to tell my wife the good news!

CHAPTER 19

The Good Life

We ultimately were in a good place. I started work with Staples in December, and my wife was already working for a different bank much closer to the house. She started there when we got the new house. That was part of the reason we were more comfortable to get a home. After my unemployment scare, I went to train in Towson. I also was asked to venture to the Bel Air store, which happened to be right across from the Office Depot. I asked not to and gave a mild explanation of why. They sent me to work in Ellicott City, far from all the ex-wife drama and craziness. When I finally arrived there, I come to find out the store manager is one of my old store managers from Office Depot, which really helped my transition to this job. We worked together up until we had a district manager change, who wanted to shake things up and fire everyone he could. Ultimately, I stuck around a short few months after he was fired but had to find somewhere else. I did that for almost a year.

I quit and started selling credit card machines. It was commissioned based, and eventually, I just couldn't sell to any new customers and had to get out. The in-laws came to visit, and we tried to enjoy a vacation while I tried to sell credit cards. We spent Halloween together, and they flew back. Our neighborhood is party central when it comes to Halloween. You can't buy enough candy for these kids.

It's been fairly quiet since the drama of the past decade and a half. I went back and finished my degree while working at a place selling Propane and Propane Accessories. I own my own home, and we throw the best parties our friends have ever had. I became an ordained minister and married K to the man of her dreams; our little own Captain Hammer look alike. Yes, things were going well. It's a terrible way to recap the years that followed the major blowup of 2013, so I'll embellish on some of the better and finer points.

In the six years since the final blow up, my ex has gone quiet. I discovered this is in part that she has been dealing with her own drama that superseded the need to hang on to me. After Latin Lover was confirmed to be out of the picture, she remarried. This second, or should I say, third dude, myself included, looked like a train wreck. A mutual friend shared wedding photos. She wore the same wedding dress from our wedding, albeit it fit a lot tighter than it did all those years ago. At that time, she had at least two kids and one miscarriage that was confirmed by my friends. Part of me thinks the miscarriage could be from when we were married. S strong part of me knows that the timeline doesn't add up, and she was never pregnant any of the time we were together.

I also came to find out that she divorced this guy just a year or so ago because he too beat on her. This seems to be a common theme. She posts on her social media pages about persevering, being strong, and not tolerating abuse. I find that ironic, all things considered. I hear she is about to walk down the aisle again, with husband number four I think. Honestly, I've lost count. Whatever floats her boat. May she find happiness with someone one day and get a daddy for all the kids she has.

I, on the other hand, am happily married now since 2012.

In April 2019, we will celebrate our seventh year of marriage. Now, even though she may drive me nuts, it's in a good way. Like how I apparently don't know how to make the bed or do laundry. The joke is on her. I know how to cook, and she still struggles in the kitchen. We have an epic relationship and have gone to comic book conventions together in costume, concerts, and other great events since we have been together. We got to see my favorite band from childhood, The Smashing Pumpkins, live on their reunion tour. She purchased the closest tickets she could find, knowing that was my favorite band.

We look out for and care for each other. We have stuck it out through so many disasters. When we first moved into the house, our water main blew, and we had to get that repaired. The plumbers blew up our electrical by hitting the main supply line and killed every single electronic item in the house. We went for almost three months with no appliances. That started at a time when I started selling propane, so I was struggling with a new job and stress. She stuck through it. Any terrible times, she knows I am there for her, and she is there for me. It's a beautiful two-way street.

She also doesn't mind I hang out with friends or that they come over. She doesn't step out at 8 PM and say they have to leave. She gets along with my friends, and as I make more they too enjoy her company. No one ever liked taking me along with my ex to places as she was such a party pooper. They love inviting the two of us together to places. Most recently, we were witness to one of my good friends' secret weddings, before the public one, where I was able to officiate for them.

I write these happy times in this chapter for two reasons. One, it's basically my closing chapter before I give my afterthoughts to everything that happened. Secondly, it's my wife's favorite number, and I know if she reads this she will probably cry. I deliberately structured the story to end on this chapter number because I truly love this woman. Even though we probably won't have children of our own, we collect cats and have each other, and that is more than anyone could ask for in this life. She completes me and works hard to ensure we have a good life, even if I make a stupid decision like quit my job and wait to start school and write a book to kill the time in between. I only hope for many more years of this absolute happiness. I thank you for joining me in this roller coaster style journey, and I doubt I'll be writing another book like this ever again.

The End.

AFTERWORD

Do books usually have one of these? I always remember seeing them. I'll take this time to get real here. Domestic Violence isn't cool. I even feel bad about the times I hurt my ex while defending myself. My advice to you if you think you want to hit someone? Go out of the house. Remove yourself from the situation. Please, for the sake of both of you: If the relationship is that toxic, consider ending the relationship calmly and civil. If you have kids, please always think of the kids. Looking at my parents' divorce, don't stick together for the sake of the kids. The less dragged out and angry it is, the easier it is on the little kids.

If you are the victim, please, don't assume this is life. Do not assume the verbal attacks, belittling, and insults are just the norm. Do not think you have to get punched in the mouth if you say something wrong. You shouldn't have to feel trapped and helpless if you find yourself in this situation. As a guy, it's really hard reaching out for help because it's assumed you are weak. Do not think that because I did for so long. If you are a lady, please, reach out to family, friends, or any agency when you feel the time is right. Do not wait too long. Get help when you can and get out as soon as possible.

Writing this story, I realized how stupid I was. But when you're living in the moment, it is really hard to see exactly what other people are trying to tell you. The signs were there since practically day one. I never listened. Looking back on my behaviors, I was just as bad by not listening to my friends and family. I was just as guilty for the things I endured. Luckily, in listening to her, I was able to step away from my life and view it from the outside. That's the only really good takeaway from my deployment.

I can't imagine what life would be like if I was dumb enough to have continued to stay with my ex. I also can't imagine my life being where it is without the events that unfolded in this book. I am angry, furious, and hurt by all the things I went through and suffer from it nightly as I am plagued with dreams. It drudged up a ton of bad memories writing this book. I already suffered from nightmares, but I was giving myself anxiety writing this. Those harmless nightmares could still be my reality. Thanks to the suggestion I needed to be in the Army, I uprooted myself and began the process of change and now have a wonderful new wife. Find your happy. We only have one life, so be sure to live your best one.

ABOUT THE AUTHOR

Harry Carpenter has been writing since elementary school. At a young age, there was always a passion for writing. Growing up has not changed those desires to write stories of his life, fiction, and other tales. Writing as a young teenager such short stories as "Dunes," he was able to develop his passion into something much greater.

His first book, "Tales From An Ex-Husband" chronicles the journey of a disastrous and toxic relationship. After much encouragement from friends and family to write a story, he did. The result is this current book you're reading. Once Harry delved back into writing, the process continued. Writing horror, sci-fi, and life stories have rekindled a love for books that he forgot he had.

Harry also is a member of the Charm City Ghostbusters, a charity organization out of Baltimore, Maryland that is dedicated to various fundraisers and events while dressed like the 1984 Hollywood Blockbuster "Ghostbusters." He also participates in a web series titled "The Web Pool," where he writes and films the majority of the sketch comedy performed by himself, Tyler Hoover and JD.

He enjoys paintball, music, and video games.

www.facebook.com/harrycarpenterwriter

BOOKS BY HARRY CARPENTER

Tales From An Ex-Husband (2019)
Spooky Stories and Scary Tales (2019)
Brain Dump (2019)

Tales From An Ex-Employee (TBA)
FUBAR - Blackout (2020)
Memoirs of a Crazed Mind (2020)
Toaster-Cop (TBA)

Thanks for reading! Please add a short review on Amazon and let me know what you thought!